# Dulcimer Songbook

by Neal Hellman


Music Sales Limited, London

**Ackowledgments**

Neal and Sally thank their friends for their help on this book: Robert Scott, Albert d'Ossché, Teddy McKnight, Robert Force, Margaret MacArthur, Roger Nicholson, Mike Rugg, Daron Douglas, Dan Rubin, Walker Fanning, Nick Hallman, Jude Goodwin, Richard Schultz, Bonnie Carol, Ruthie Dorenfeld, and Kevin Roth.

**Photo Credits**

Technical photos by Sol Hellman
P. 37 - Carl Fleischhauer
P. 57 - Albert d'Ossché
P. 60, 75 - Herb Wise
P. 67, 83 - Bonnie Carol
P. 73 - John Merrill
Front cover photo - Bonnie Carol
Back cover photo - Laura Benson

Book and cover design by Barbara B. Hoffman
All musical timing in the tablature by Sally Hellman



International Standard Book Number: 0-8256-0191-6
Library of Congress Catalog Card Number: 77-79697

Music Sales Limited
78 Newman Street, W1 London

Music Sales (Pty) Limited
27 Clarendon Street, Artarmon, Sydney NSW, Australia

Music Sales Corporation
4-26-22 Jingumae, Shibuya-ku, Tokyo 150 Japan

# Contents

# Introduction

Within the last decade the dulcimer has had a virtual renaissance in North America. A great number of books have been released and dulcimers have become stock items in music stores; dulcimer-makers cannot fill all their orders. There is a new magazine, *Dulcimer Player News*, and dulcimer festivals held yearly. Dulcimers are appearing on contemporary albums and in concert halls. People are using the dulcimer in new areas of music, as McCoy Tyner does in his jazz piece "Mode for Dulcimer" on his album *Focal Point*. The realization that the dulcimer is not a limited instrument has greatly helped its new popularity. The purpose of this book is to stimulate and expand players' awareness of the dulcimer.

Many people still believe that the dulcimer can only be played in the mode and key it's tuned to. One of the main points in this book is to show the player *how to play in many modes without retuning the strings.* When tuned to the standard Mixolydian Mode, for example, one can play in five different modes and keys without retuning. This valuable technique can be used in almost all the other diatonic modes.

With the aid of a homemade *capo* one can play in *all* the modes and keys without retuning the strings. Learning how to change all the modes and keys without stopping will greatly enhance the ability to play with other people.

The dulcimer can also be used as a back-up instrument on fast fiddle tunes and ballads. Many is the time I've seen a dulcimer laid down at a jam session when the pace got too fast. But one does not have to play every note of a tune to play along with other instruments. The dulcimer sounds beautiful when simple chords are played around a fast jig or reel. The drone aspect of the dulcimer surrounds a melody line and gives a tune added depth and rhythm.

By realizing the above two techniques of changing modes one can play along with fast medleys that change keys between tunes.

People are also now discovering the beauty of fingerpicking the dulcimer. Someone who has never fingerpicked the instrument before will be surprised at the beautiful melodic patterns that can be created. Try different fingerpicking styles with a tune you know fairly well.

As well as a book on technique this is also a collection of my favorite tunes and ballads. To illustrate the above methods I have chosen fifty-five compositions.

One can play more than just traditional American music on the dulcimer. Only a small percentage of the tunes here are of the Appalachian genre. Irish and English jigs and reels, Scottish airs, hornpipes, step dances, and contemporary music can be found within the pages of this book.

It is my hope that after reading and playing this book you will feel like composing your own music on the dulcimer.

# I. Modes and Tunings

There are seven different modes to which you can tune your dulcimer, and within each of these modes there are several ways to tune. Before examining the various tunings, let's first understand the concept of a *keytone.*

A keytone is the *tonic note* of the key you wish to tune to (D for the key of D, or E for the key of E), determined by the tension of the string that feels good (neither too loose nor too tight) and the pitch that suits your voice.

## The Ionian Mode

You can play the Ionian Mode scale on any string by starting on the 3rd fret.

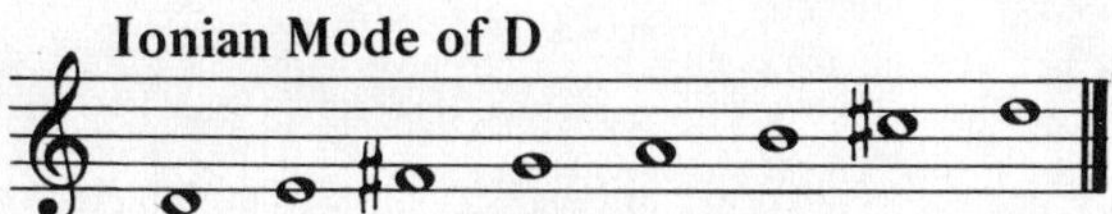


Tune your bass string (the string furthest from you), to the desired keytone. Press down on the 4th fret (actually, just to the left) of the bass string and tune the other two or three strings an octave above the note. AA-A-D, GG-G-C are examples of Ionian Mode tunings in D and C respectively (from left to right: high to low strings–double letters are melody strings). All Ionian tunings are looked on as Major key tunings. The D Ionian Mode would give us the key of D Major, C would give us C Major, and so on.

*New Ionian tuning:* Due to differing tensions of the strings many people find it hard to tune to the standard modes. If your strings keep breaking in the Ionian Mode or any standard mode, simply use your *middle string* for the desired keytone. The bass then takes the value of the old middle string note and the melody string(s) stay the same. DD-G-D (key of G) and GG-C-G (key of C) are examples of New Ionian Tunings.

Therefore, if you have trouble with string tension for any standard mode, try using the middle string as your desired keytone. Also, if you see tunes in the book written out for the New Mixolydian or the Standard Dorian Tunings and you want to do them in Standard Mixolydian or New Dorian, respectively, simply reverse the middle and bass strings of the tablature.

*Other Ionian tunings:* AA-D-D, DD-G-D or DD-G-B; the first is a D tuning and the other two are G tunings.

## The Mixolydian Mode

A very important and versatile mode. The Mixolydian Mode scale is played on each string starting on the open note.

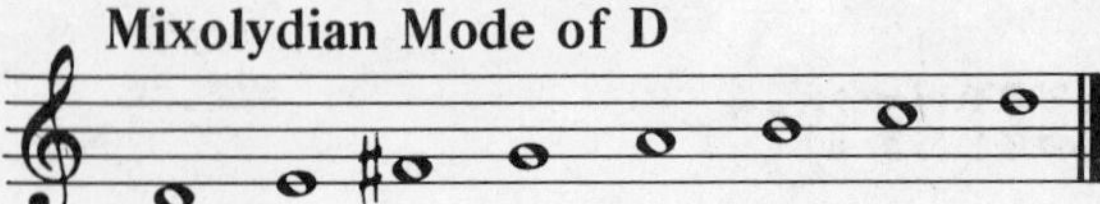


Tune the bass to the desired keytone. Then tune the melody string an octave above. Press the 4th fret of the bass and tune the middle string an octave above. DD-A-D and CC-G-C are standard Mixolydian tunings for D and C respectively.

*New Mixolydian tunings:* AA-A-E (key of A), GG-C-D (key of G), DA-A-D (key of D).

*Other Mixolydian tunings:* AA-A-A' an octave below (key of A–sometimes called "bagpipe tuning"). DE-A-D (key of D), CD-G-C (key of C).

## The Aeolian Mode

Used for minor keys–the scale is played on each string starting on the 1st fret.

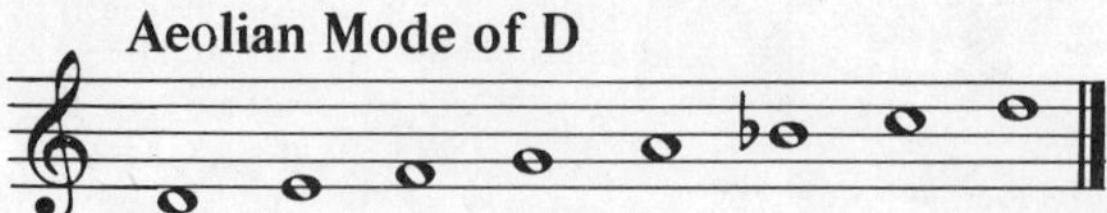


Tune your bass string to the desired keytone. Press down the 4th fret and tune your middle string an octave above it. Then press the 6th fret of the bass string and tune the melody strings an octave above that. Common tunings are: GG-E-A (Aeolian of A, or Am), AA-F♯-B (Aeolian of B, or Bm).

*New Aeolian tunings:* GG-A-E (Am), CC-D-A (Dm), DD-B-B (B Aeolian), etc.

## The Dorian Mode

This also can be used for minor keys–for each string the scale starts on the 4th fret.

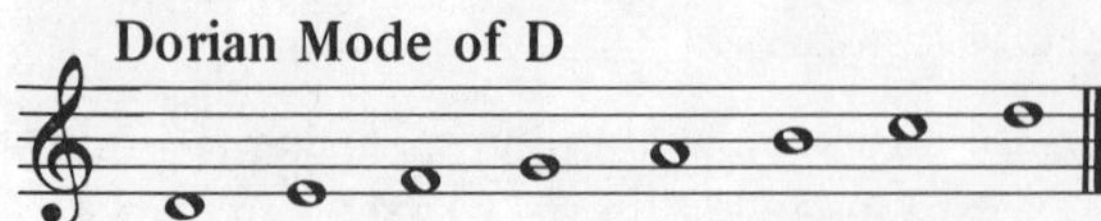


Tune your bass string to the desired keytone. Press the 4th fret of the bass and the middle string an octave above. Then play the 3rd fret of the bass and tune the first string an octave above. Standard tunings: GG-A-D (Dorian of D, or Dm), CC-D-G (Dorian of G, or Gm).

*New Dorian tunings:* GG-D-G (Dm), AA-E-B (Em).

*Other Dorian tunings:* DD-A-A (Am), CC-G-G (Gm).

## The Lydian Mode

Similar to the Ionian but has a sharped 4th—the scale is played on each string starting on the 6th fret.

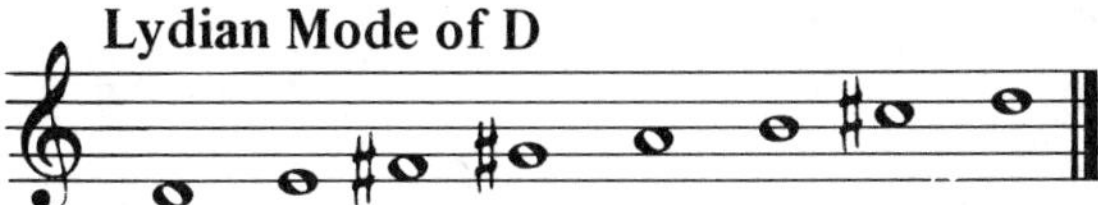


Tune bass to the desired keytone; press the 1st fret and tune the melody strings an octave above it. Then press the bass at the 4th fret and tune the middle string an octave above that. Standard tunings: DD-G-C (Lydian of C), EE-A-D (Lydian of D).

*New Lydian tunings:* AA-G-D (Lydian of G), EE-D-A (Lydian of D), etc.

## The Phrygian Mode

Can be used for minor keys—the scale is played on each string starting at the 5th fret.

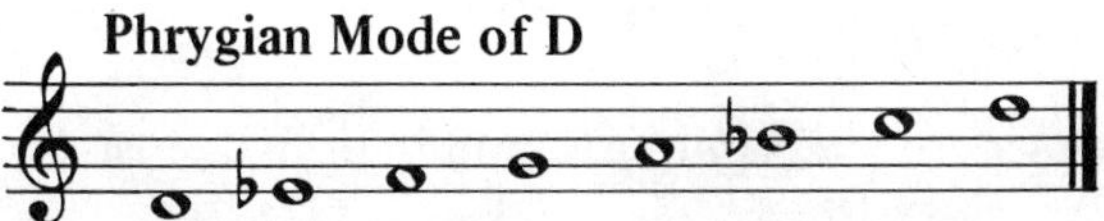


Tune the bass to the desired keytone, and press at the 4th fret, tuning all the other strings an octave above it. Then press the first string (melody) at the 2nd fret and tune it down so that at that fret it matches the open second string. This lowers the melody strings to a minor third below the second string. Common tunings: FF-A-D (Phrygian of D), E♭E♭-G-C (Phrygian of C).

*New Phrygian tuning:* FF-D-A (Phrygian of D).

## The Locrian Mode

Can be used for minor keys—this scale begins on the 2nd fret for each string.

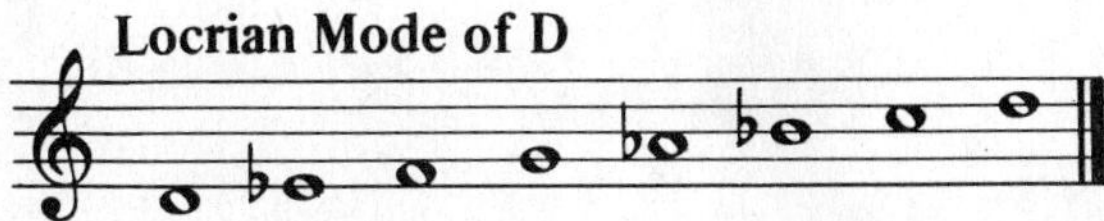


Due to its strange scale (½-step, step, step, ½-step, step, step, step) this mode has hardly ever been employed in western music. However, one can work out some really nice things with it. (Those who have the extra fret (6½) on their dulcimers will find it most handy in this mode.) It sounds very oriental, and makes a very fine mode for your evening meditation.

This time tune the melody strings to the desired keytone. Press down the melody string at the 2nd fret and tune the bass string an octave below it. Then press the bass at the 4th fret and tune the middle string an octave above it. B♭ B♭ -A-D (D Locrian), AA-G♯-C♯ (C♯ Locrian). Even though the middle strings here are not actually in the mode (A is not in D Locrian, nor G♯ in C♯), they make an effective drone as you play the melody strings.

*New Locrian tuning:* E♭ E♭-G-D (Locrian of D).
In the next chapter (p. 12) we will explore ways of playing in various modes without having to retune the strings.

## Stringing Your Dulcimer

There are numerous ways to string a dulcimer. No matter what type of string (banjo , guitar, etc.) you put on the dulcimer I would advise knowing the gauge (thickness) of the string you use. By knowing the gauge one can know the limits of the string. For example, a .010 will not hit a high G, while a .009 will. Companies like *Ernie Ball* and *G.H.S.* sell strings separately, so you'll know exactly what you're putting on the instrument. If you buy dulcimer strings in sets be sure they tell the gauge on the package. You should always try to use a bronze wound bass string. Also be sure to note if your dulcimer takes loop or ball end strings before you go to the store.

There appear to be two popular ways to string a dulcimer:

*Stringing Method no. 1:* Where the melody strings are the same, the middle a little heavier and a wound bass is used: .010, .010-.012, .022W.

If using banjo strings: 2 second strings, 1 third, 1 fourth.

If using guitar strings: 2 first strings, 1 second, 1 third.

The following tuning chart can be utilized with the above strings. Start from DD-A-D:

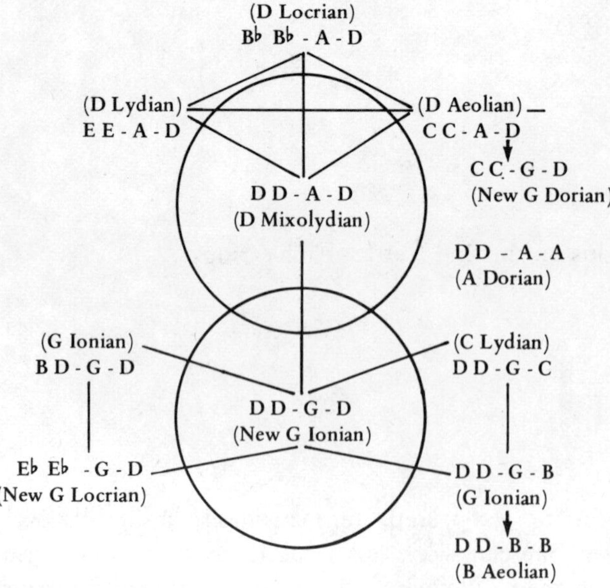

*String Method no. 2:* Where the upper strings are the same gauge and the bass is a wound string: .014-.014, .014, .022W.

If using banjo: 3 thirds and a fourth.

If using guitar strings: 3 seconds and 1 third.

The following tunings are possible with the above strings:

AA-D-D (D Ionian).
AA-A-D (D Ionian) or FF-A-D (D Phrygian) or B♭B♭-A-D (D Locrian).
AA-A-E (New Mix. of A) or AA-A-A (A "Bagpipe") or GG-A-E (New Aeolian of A).
AA-B-E (Dorian of E) or BB-B-E (E Ionian).
AA-B-F♯ (New B Aeolian).

There are of course many other ways to string a dulcimer. Experiment with different gauges and types till you find some that you like.

## Musical Symbols

Even if you already read music, you should find this section useful. If you don't read, don't be dismayed; most of the music here is in tablature, and there's a lot less here to understand about standard music notation than in most music books.

The only time we use actual *notes* in this book is for the songs with words. This is so you'll know how the vocal part is sung (sometimes the dulcimer plays a slightly different melody from the one you sing).

Look at the first tune, "Bonaparte's Retreat," p. 18 . The notes under the tablature determine the timing of each composition. When you don't play anything you'll see a sign called a *rest.* This chart shows the time values of both notes and rests:

| | **Rest** | **Note** | *Count (in 2/4, 3/4, or 4/4)* |
|---|---|---|---|
| **Whole:** | 𝄻 | 𝅝 | *4 beats. Count: 1 - and 2 - and 3 - and 4 - and* |
| **Half:** | 𝄼 | 𝅗𝅥 | *2 beats. Count: 1 - and 2 - and* |
| **Quarter:** | 𝄽 | ♩ | *1 beat. Count: 1 - and* |
| **Eighth:** | 𝄾 | ♪ | *1/2 beat. Count: (1-).* |
| **Sixteenth:** | 𝄿 | 𝅘𝅥𝅯 | *1/4 beat. ( 𝅘𝅥𝅯 𝅘𝅥𝅯 =1-)* |

Sixteenth notes and eighth notes can be joined together by a *beam:*

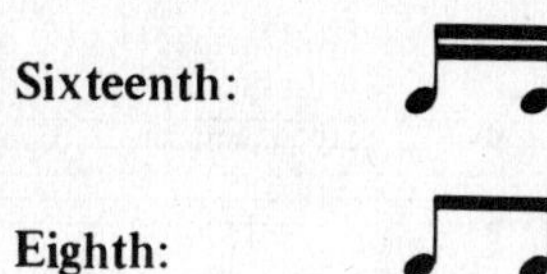

A dot after a note means you hold it 1½ times the value of the original note:

𝅝· = *6 beats.*

𝅗𝅥· = *3 beats.*

♩· = *1½ beats (1 – and 2 –).*

It helps if you count the beats out loud when you first play a new song.

Each song is divided into sections called *measures* which are separated by *barlines*:

**time signature:**

| bar | 0 | 3 | 3 | bar |
|---|---|---|---|---|
| **3** | 0 | 3 | 3 | |
| **4** | 2 | 3 | 4 | |
| | ♩ | ♩ | ♩ | |

← measure →

The number of beats in each measure is written out at the beginning of each song in the *time signature*: ¾ in this song. The top number tells you how many beats per measure, and the bottom number tells you the time value of each beat.

3  3 beats per measure.
4  every quarter (1/4) note counts as one beat.

6  6 beats per measure.
8  every eighth (1/8) note counts as one beat.

A lot of tunes in this book are divided by repeat signs:

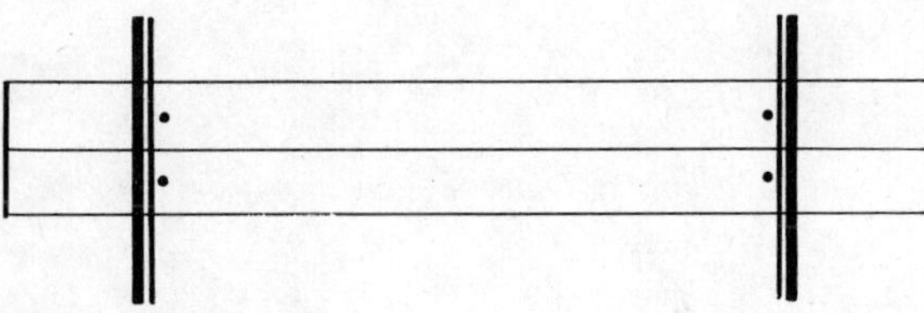

These mean that you repeat everything between them *once* before you go on to the next part.

*The staff*: As mentioned above, for the songs in this book with words we've written out a staff, so you'll know how the vocal melody goes.

A staff is a set of 5 lines; each line and each space between the lines stands for one note; this includes lines drawn above or below the staff (ledger lines). The staff below has a *treble clef*; this means the note-pitches are as shown. A different clef sign (*bass* or *alto)* would put the notes at a lower pitch-level.

When a note falls above or below the staff you just keep drawing ledger lines to fit that note in. "Middle C" on a piano is 1 extra line below the regular staff, a high "A" would be one extra line above it, etc.

To tell what key a song is in, one looks at the beginning of the staff to see how many sharps (♯) or flats (♭) the song has. A sharp is a half-step above the original note, a flat is a half-step below. Note that a sharped note is usually the same as the flatted note just above it; that is, G♯ =A♭ , D♯=E♭, etc. (The exceptions to this are: B♯=C♮, E♯ =F♮; C♭=B♮, F♭=E♮.)

A song in the Key of D Major which has 2 sharps (F♯ and C♯ ) would look like this:

| Key | Number of Sharps or Flats |
|---|---|
| C and Am | None |
| D and Bm | F♯ and C♯ |
| E and C♯m | F♯, C♯, G♯ and D♯ |
| F and Dm | B♭ |
| G and Em | F♯ |
| A and F♯m | F♯, C♯ and G♯ |
| B♭ and Gm | B♭ and E♭ |

If a song contains a sharp or flat that isn't normally in that key, it is written directly in front of the note it refers to:

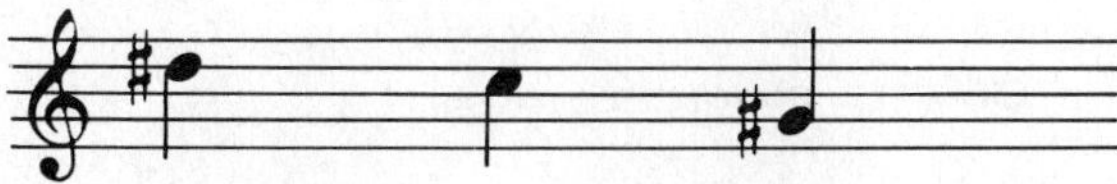

All the same notes inside that measure would be sharp, but once you start a new measure (unless there is a new sharp sign) you would go back to playing the original note. The same thing happens if you need to play a "natural" note in a key where that note would normally be sharp. A "natural" sign (♮) would be written in front of the note.

On the dulcimer, due to its diatonic scale, we sometimes have a song where one of the sharps in the tune will be played natural throughout the song. "A Maid That's Deep In Love" (p. 86 ) is a perfect example. The vocal (musical staff) is written out for the key of A Major (F♯ , C♯ and G♯). However, when the dulcimer is tuned to a Mixolydian Mode of A (AA-A-E) we have no G♯ on the melody string. By placing a natural sign at the beginning of each line we save the trouble of placing this sign on every G note.

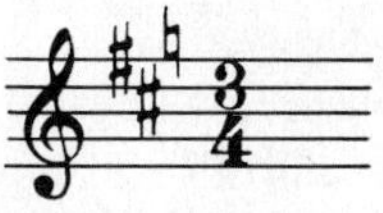

# II. Changing Modes and Keys Without Retuning the Strings

## Changing Modes in Standard Mixolydian Tuning

For convenience and ease in playing we will use the DD-A-D tuning (Standard Mixolydian tuning in D) for this and the next chapter. *Any* standard Mixolydian tuning will work, so if you use a different one, say: CC-G-C or AA-E-A, simply *transpose* every chord, note, position and key you see here. This transposing will be an effortless process once you've retuned, since the fretting of the chords will be the same.

By utilizing the proper chord positions one can play very well in the modes and keys of D, G, Em and Bm, and can manage in A, all the while being tuned to DD-A-D.* First, let's write out the chords and their positions, and then utilize them in the context of some tunes.

### Chord Positions in DD-A-D Tuning

**D Chords:**

| | | | | | | | | | |
|---|---|---|---|---|---|---|---|---|---|
| 0 | 0 | 0 | 0 | 2 | 0 | 4 | 0 | 7 | 7 |
| 0 | 0 | 0 | 3 | 3 | 5 | 5 | 7 | 0 | 7 |
| 0 | 2 | 4 | 4 | 4 | 7 | 7 | 7 | 7 | 9 |

**C Chords:**

| | | | | | | |
|---|---|---|---|---|---|---|
| 6 | 3 | 6 | 0 | 6 | 8 | *bass string* |
| 6 | 4 | 4 | 6 | 6 | 6 | *middle string* |
| 8 | 6 | 6 | 6 | 0 | 6 | *melody string(s)* |

**G Chords:**

| | | | | | |
|---|---|---|---|---|---|
| 0 | 3 | 3 | 7 | 5 | 7 |
| 1 | 3 | 3 | 6 | 6 | 8 |
| 3 | 3 | 5 | 5 | 7 | 10 |

**A Chords:**

| | | | | | | | |
|---|---|---|---|---|---|---|---|
| 1 | 1 | 4 | 0 | 0 | 8 | 8 | 4 |
| 0 | 2 | 4 | 4 | 2 | 7 | 0 | 4 |
| 1 | 1 | 4 | 4 | 4 | 8 | 8 | 6½ |

**E Chords:**

| | |
|---|---|
| | 8 |
| 1 | 8 |
| 1 | 8 |

**Em Chords:**

| | | | | |
|---|---|---|---|---|
| 1 | 1 | 3 | 5 | 5 |
| 1 | 1 | 4 | 4 | 6 |
| 1 | 3 | 5 | 3 | 8 |

**Am Chords:**

| | | | |
|---|---|---|---|
| 4 | 4 | 6 | 4 |
| 4 | 4 | 7 | 4 |
| 4 | 5 | 8 | 6 |

| Bm Chords: | | | | F♯m | Cm7th | Dm7th | Am7th |
|---|---|---|---|---|---|---|---|
| 0 | 5 | 5 | 5 | 2 | 3 | 0 | 4 |
| 1 | 5 | 5 | 5 | 2 | 1 | 2 | 2 |
| 2 | 5 | 7 | 0 | 2 | 2 | 2 | 3 |

Since the bass string is the same pitch as the melody (an octave lower) one can *invert* any of the above chords. 0/3/4 can be 4/3/0 and so on. There are even more chord possibilites, but this should be enough to get you started.

Now let's turn to the tunes and see how these chords can give us different keys and modes without retuning the strings.

*In C Standard Mixolydian tuning (CC-G-C) you can play in C, F, Dm, Gm and G. In E Mixolydian (EE-B-E) you can play in E, F m, A, Bm and B. And so on for other Mixolydian Modes.

# The Tablature in This Book

One will notice that the tablature will vary a bit among the many tunes and ballads within this chapter. Let's look at a simple tab like "The Eighth of January," (p. 19):

–The 3 lines represent the three strings of the dulcimer, with the melody strings on the bottom and the bass on top.
–The numbers represent which fret you push down.
–The notes on the bottom are for the timing of the piece.
–The chords written on top of the dulcimer tab are there to help you use the dulcimer as a "back-up" instrument. The fretting of each chord is shown above the tune.

Many of the songs, like "The Eighth of January," are in two versions, a "melody" version (in tab) and a "back-up" version (chords above the tab). Although throughout the chapter we will explore different modes and keys, the key will always be the same within each composition for both back-up and melody. However, the *tunings* for the two versions may be different. So even though most of the back-up chord-parts in this chapter are written for standard Mixolydian tuning in D (DD-A-D), the chords themselves may be in some other mode than Mixolydian. In other words, you may be playing chords in the Aeolian mode, but your dulcimer is tuned in standard Mixolydian D tuning. This happens in "Tarbolton Lodge," p. 22 , for example. But, for the melody version of "Tarbolton Lodge," the dulcimer is tuned to Aeolian (DD-B-E). So although the *tuning* for the two versions is different, the *sound* is the same mode (Aeolian). You and a friend can play both versions together, with one playing the back-up chords in Mixolydian D tuning and the other playing the melody version in Aeolian tuning.

The first three songs in this chapter, "Bonaparte's Retreat," "The Eighth of January," and "Patsy Campbell" are in the Mixolydian Mode (chord and melody versions are both for Mixolydian tuning, DD-A-D). In the next tune, "Swallowtail Jig," the melody version is given in the Dorian mode and in Dorian tuning (AA-B-E), but the chords are in Mixolydian D tuning. "The Black Nag" (p. 23 ) has the melody in the E Aeolian mode and the chords once again in Mixolydian D tuning. And so on.

Just be aware of which mode the melody is in, and read each heading carefully for tuning and other information.

On all the sung ballads (songs) there is a musical staff in standard notation given above the lyrics. Sometimes the dulcimer part varies somewhat from the melody of the song. The staff is written out so one can be sure of the melody of the composition (as in "C'est l'aviron," p. 26).

# Playing the Chords

The first thing I would suggest in making the chords is to choose whatever feels good. I will illustrate a few here to give you some ideas.

First, it depends on what position you play the dulcimer in. There seem to be three basic positions:

1. Sitting down with the dulcimer on your lap.

2. Sitting or standing up, playing the dulcimer over the top.

3. Sitting or standing, playing the dulcimer from underneath like a guitar.

Let's take a simple chord like 0/0/2. In position no. 1 you'd fret the melody string with your thumb, index or middle finger. The same goes for position no. 2. However, if you're using position no. 3 you might try the 2nd fret of the bass string, since it's the same note. Remember that in the DD-A-D tuning the first and bass string are interchangeable.

Let's take a chord like 4/4/4. One can barre it with just one finger, or use your three middle fingers to cover the frets. It all depends on the tune and where you have to move next. For example, in "Forest of Garth" (p. 29 ) it's better to use 3 fingers in position no. 1, but it's beneficial to use 1 finger (barre) when playing in position no. 3.*

Let's take the last run in "The Swallowtail Jig" (p. 21) to illustrate our various positions.

The chords we play are:

First, *sitting down as in Position no. 1,* start with the $G^1$ (5-6-7) chord:

- –Place your ring finger on the 5th fret of the first string.
- –Middle finger on the 6th fret of the middle string.
- –Index finger on the 7th fret of the bass string.

Now just slide the whole assembly down three frets and we have the $D^2$ (2-3-4) chord. Then slide all three fingers up to the 3rd fret, in a different chord position, and we have the $G^2$ (3-3-3) chord. Now lift them all up and strum the open dulcimer for the $D^3$ (0-0-0) chord. Then use the same three fingers to cover the lst fret of all three strings for the Em (1-1-1) and you've got it.

**The Swallowtail Jig–Position no. 1**

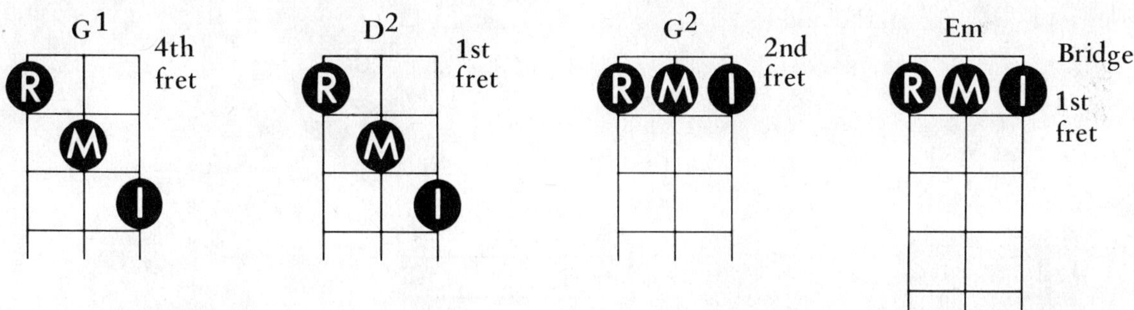


Now let's try the same run from *underneath–Position no. 3,* starting once again with the $G^1$ chord.

- –Place your pinky on the 7th fret of the bass string.
- –Middle finger on the 6th fret of the middle string.
- –Barre the entire 5th fret with your index finger.

*In some of the "back-up" tunes we might see some odd chord names like $D^2$, $G^1$, or $D^3$. These numbers given to the chords show the order of appearance of the chords in the tune. D would be the first D chord used in the tune; $D^2$ would be the third D chord used, and so on. A $D^1$ in one tune might be $D^2$ in another. Check the chord fingerings given with each tune to avoid confusion.

For the $D^2$ chord we merely slide the whole assembly down till your index finger is barring the 2nd fret, your middle finger is on the 3rd fret of the middle string, and your pinky is on the 4th fret of the bass string. Then barre the entire 3rd fret with your index finger to make the $G^2$ chord, leave the strings open for the $D^3$ chord and then barre the entire lst fret for the Em chord. Once you have this technique mastered you will be able to accompany almost any tune in Em in Position no. 3.

**The Swallowtail Jig—Position no. 3**

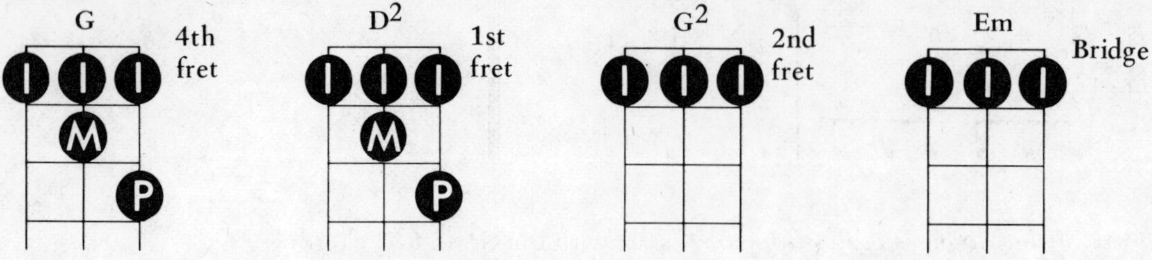


To play *over the top of the dulcimer (Position no. 2)* we have a pattern similar to Position no. 3. In this case we use our ring finger to do all the barring, our middle-finger position remains the same, and we fret the melody string(s) with our index finger instead of fretting the bass string with our pinky as in the previous example. Albert d'Ossché and Bob Force play the dulcimer in this manner.

All the chords with the middle string open and with matching frets on the melody and bass (4-0-4, 6-0-6) can be done with the thumb on the melody and the index finger on the bass string.

On chords where the middle string is fretted and either the melody string or the bass (but not both) is open (0-1-2, 6-5-0), try using your index finger on the bass or melody string and your middle finger on the middle string.

Lastly, let's look at the first few measures of "Maggie in the Wood" (p. 25):

**G Ionian Mode**
**Part A**
Tuning

| Tuning | 2/4 | | | | | | | | | | | | | | |
|---|---|---|---|---|---|---|---|---|---|---|---|---|---|---|---|
| D | | 3 | 3 | 3 | 3 | 3 | 3 | 5 | 6 | 6 | 6 | 6 | 5 | |
| A | | 3 | 3 | 3 | 3 | 3 | 3 | 6 | 6 | 6 | 6 | 6 | 6 | |
| DD | | 3 | 0 | 3 | 3 | 4 | 5 | 7 | 8 | 10 | 9 | 8 | 7 | etc. |

In Position no. 1, for the first G chord in the A part (3-3-3) try:

—Ring finger on the 3rd fret of the melody string.
—Middle finger on the 3rd fret of the middle string.
—Index finger on the 3rd fret of the bass string.

So for the 4-3-3 chord and the 5-3-3 chord we merely slide the thumb. 7-6-5 is the thumb-index-middle respectively. Now, on the 8-6-6 chord, your thumb is on the melody string and your index and middle are both on the 6th fret of the middle and bass strings. Following the same rules, the "B" part should pose no problem.

**Maggie in the Wood—Position no. 1**

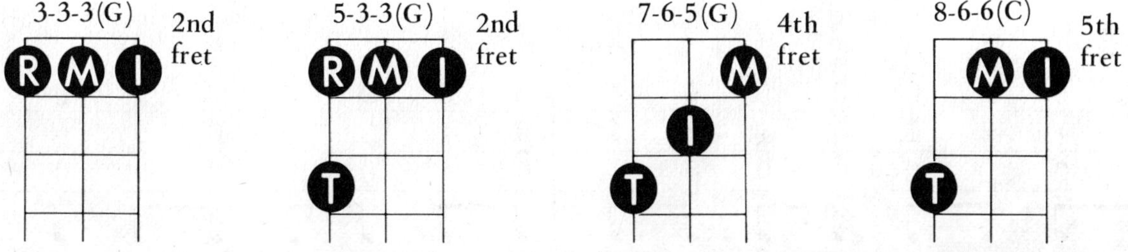


Further instruction will appear with each tune. If it seems difficult at first, just concentrate on one tune, one that you've heard before. Once you've got these chording techniques together you'll be able to accompany fast fiddlers playing medleys that change key: jigs, reels, hornpipes, and whatever else you like.

**A Few More Chords—Position no. 1**

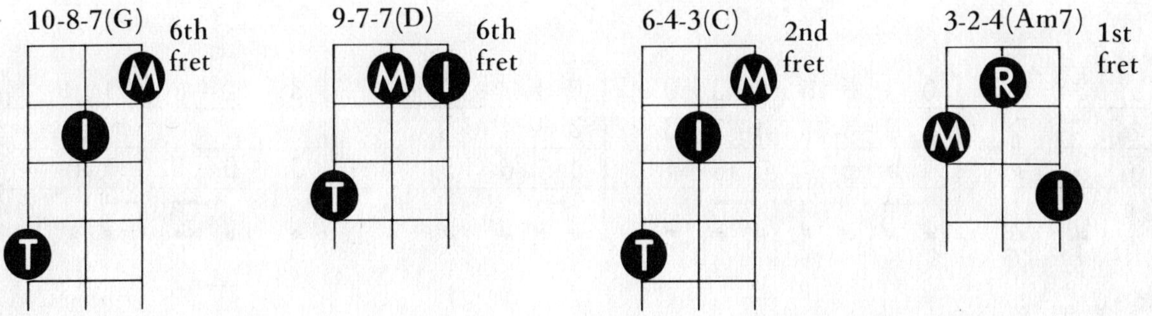

## BONAPARTE'S RETREAT

Tune to the standard Mixolydian of D (DD-A-D). Remember to play each part twice. Notice the harmonic in the "A" part, marked "*harm.*"; it is for all the strings.

Traditional
Arranged by Neal and Sally Hellman

**Part A**

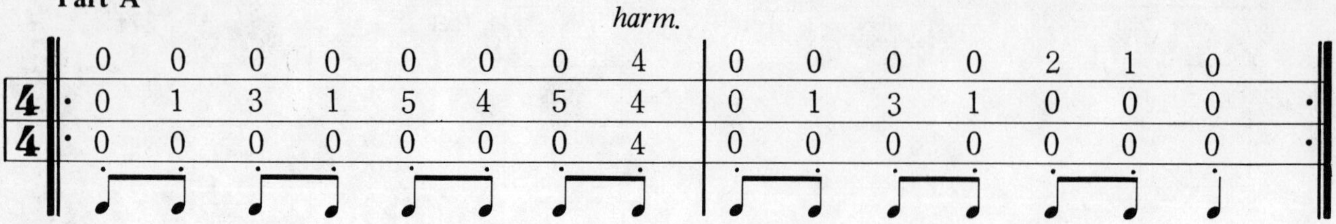

*harm.*

4/4

| 0 | 0 | 0 | 0 | 0 | 0 | 0 | 4 | 0 | 0 | 0 | 0 | 2 | 1 | 0 |
|---|---|---|---|---|---|---|---|---|---|---|---|---|---|---|
| 0 | 1 | 3 | 1 | 5 | 4 | 5 | 4 | 0 | 1 | 3 | 1 | 0 | 0 | 0 |
| 0 | 0 | 0 | 0 | 0 | 0 | 0 | 4 | 0 | 0 | 0 | 0 | 0 | 0 | 0 |

**Part B**

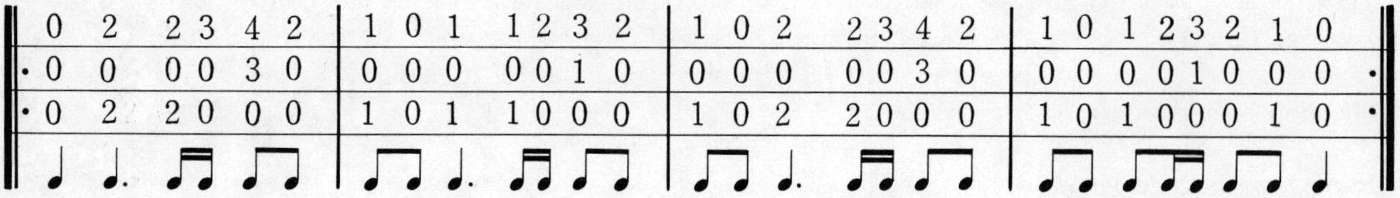

| 0 2 23 4 2 | 1 0 1 1232 | 1 0 2 2342 | 1 0 1232 1 0 |
|---|---|---|---|
| 0 0 00 3 0 | 0 0 0 0010 | 0 0 0 0030 | 0 0 0010 0 0 |
| 0 2 20 0 0 | 1 0 1 1000 | 1 0 2 2000 | 1 0 1000 1 0 |

**Part C**

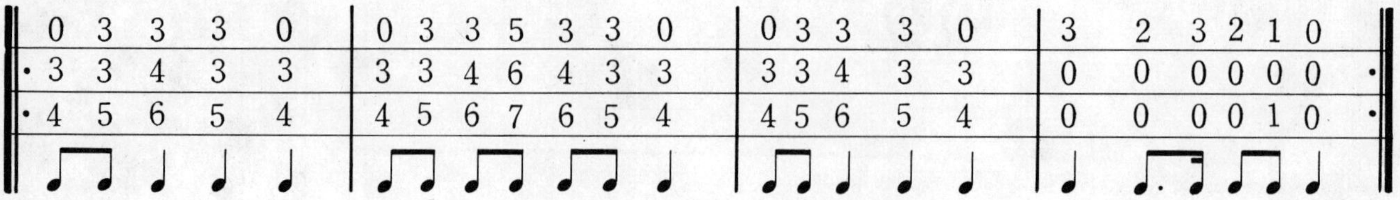

| 0 3 3 3 0 | 0 3 3 5 3 3 0 | 0 3 3 3 0 | 3 2 3 2 1 0 |
|---|---|---|---|
| 3 3 4 3 3 | 3 3 4 6 4 3 3 | 3 3 4 3 3 | 0 0 0 0 0 0 |
| 4 5 6 5 4 | 4 5 6 7 6 5 4 | 4 5 6 5 4 | 0 0 0 0 1 0 |

# THE EIGHTH OF JANUARY

Tune to the Mixolydian of D (DD-A-D). Both the chordal and the note-for-note, melodic way of playing the piece are given. I would suggest playing the back-up chords in the "A" part and the melody version in the "B" part. I did not bother writing out the chords for the "B" part because it sounds so good just to play the melody. Since the bass string is the same note as the melody, try inverting any chords or playing the melody part on the bass string. One may use any of the positions for the chords, but I suggest for starters:

```
     0        0        1
G =  1   D =  0   A =  0
     3        2        1
```

Next try these:

```
     0        5        7        0
D =  5   G =  6   or   6   A =  4
     7        7        5        4
```

Traditional
Arranged by Neal and Sally Hellman

**Part A**
Back-up chords:

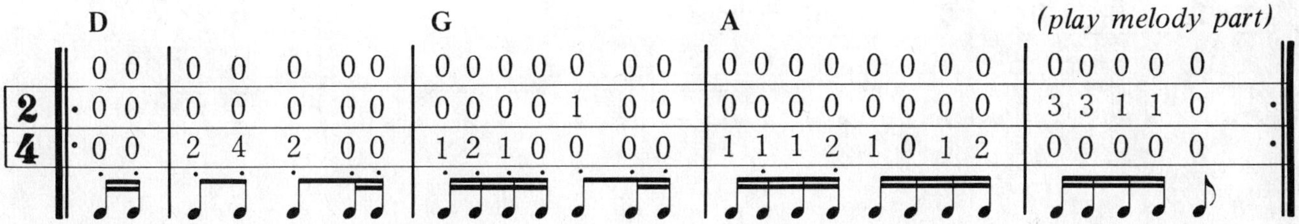

```
      D                     G                    A                    (play melody part)
 ||  0 0 | 0 0  0 0 0 | 0 0 0 0 0  0 0 | 0 0 0 0 0 0 0 0 | 0 0 0 0 0   ||
2||: 0 0 | 0 0  0 0 0 | 0 0 0 0 1  0 0 | 0 0 0 0 0 0 0 0 | 3 3 1 1 0  :||
4||: 0 0 | 2 4  2 0 0 | 1 2 1 0 0  0 0 | 1 1 1 2 1 0 1 2 | 0 0 0 0 0  :||
```

**Melody &/or voice**

**Part B**

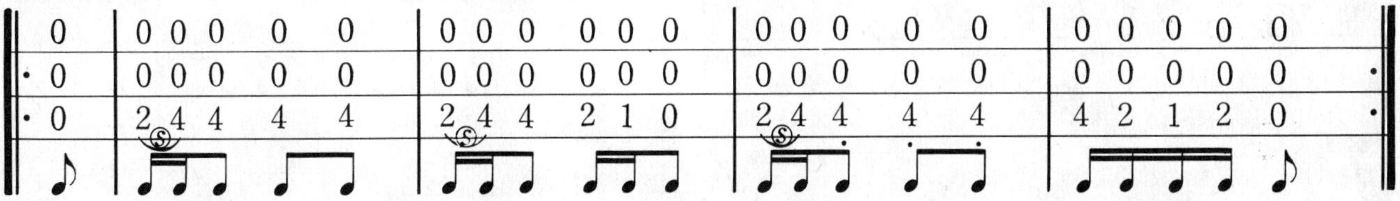

```
 ||  0 | 0 0 0  0 0 | 0 0 0  0 0 0 | 0 0 0  0 0 | 0 0 0 0 0   ||
 ||: 0 | 0 0 0  0 0 | 0 0 0  0 0 0 | 0 0 0  0 0 | 0 0 0 0 0  :||
 ||: 0 | 2 4 4  4 4 | 2 4 4  2 1 0 | 2 4 4  4 4 | 4 2 1 2 0  :||
            (S)          (S)            (S)
```

# PATSY CAMPBELL

Stay tuned to the D Mixolydian (DD-A-D). Both chords and melody are in D Mixolydian Mode.

| | D1 | D2 | C1 | G1 | C2 | A | G2 |
|---|---|---|---|---|---|---|---|
| | 0 | 0 | 6 | 3 | 6 | 4 | 5 |
| = | 5 | 3 | 6 | 1 | 4 | 4 | 3 |
| | 4 | 2 | 6 | 0 | 3 | 4 | 3 |

Traditional
In the style of Walker Fanning

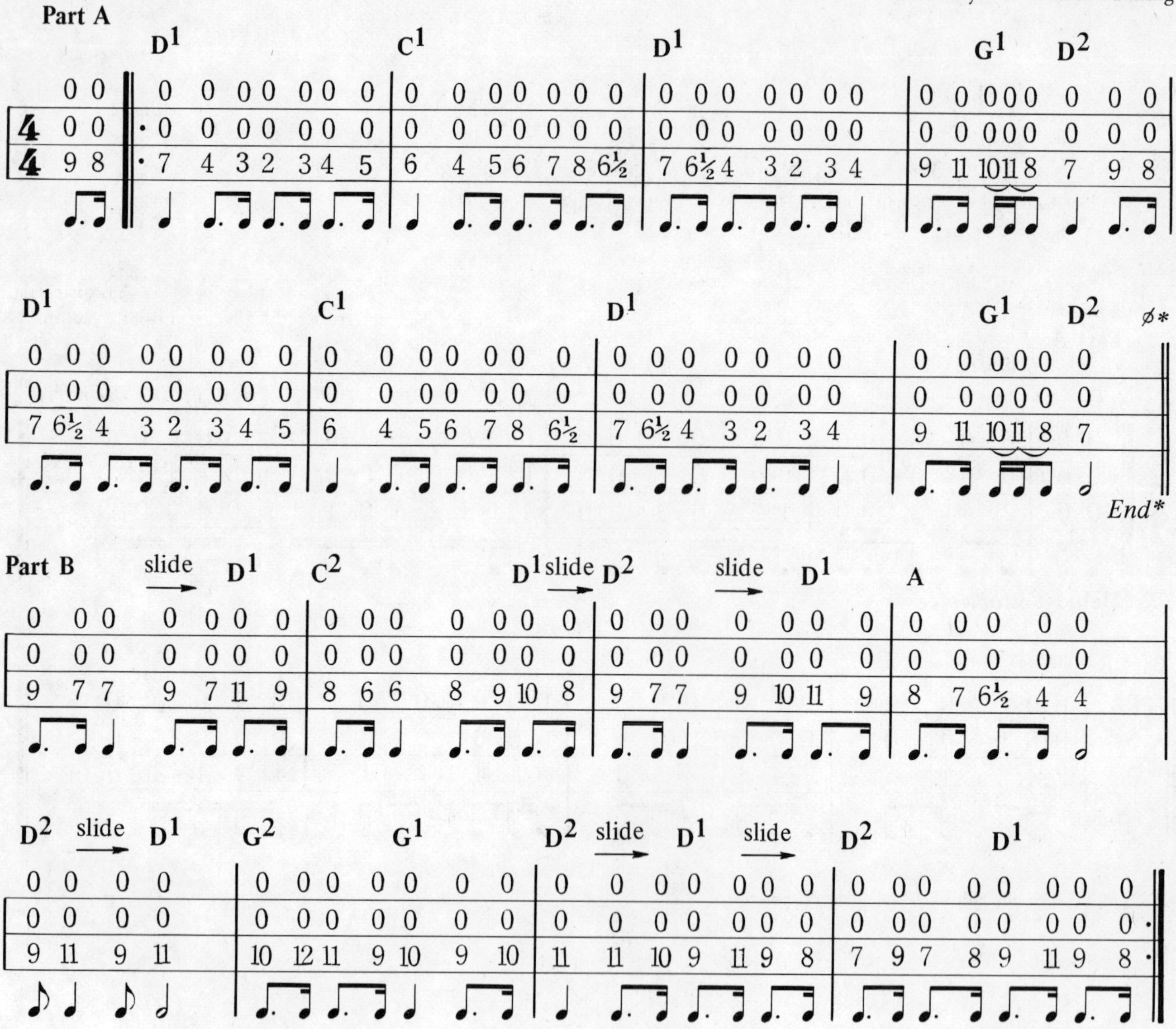

**Part A**

```
          D1                    C1                    D1                  G1        D2
   0 0 || 0  0 00 00 0  | 0  0 00 00 0  | 0 0 0  00 00 | 0 0000  0  0 0 |
4  0 0 ||·0  0 00 00 0  | 0  0 00 00 0  | 0 0 0  00 00 | 0 0000  0  0 0 |
4  9 8 ||·7  4 32 34 5  | 6  4 56 78 6½ | 7 6½4  32 34 | 9 11 1011 8  7  9 8 |

D1                    C1                    D1                  G1       D2     ∅*
0 00 00 000 | 0  0 00 00 0  | 0 00 00 00 | 0 0000 0 ||
0 00 00 000 | 0  0 00 00 0  | 0 00 00 00 | 0 0000 0 ||
7 6½4 32 345 | 6  4 56 78 6½ | 7 6½4 32 34 | 9 11 1011 8 7 ||
                                                          End*
```

**Part B**

```
     slide D1        C2          D1 slide D2      slide D1          A
0 00  0 00 0  | 0 00  0 00 0    | 0 00  0 00 0     | 0 00 00 |
0 00  0 00 0  | 0 00  0 00 0    | 0 00  0 00 0     | 0 00 00 |
9 77  9 711 9 | 8 66  8 910 8   | 9 77  9 1011 9   | 8 76½ 44 |

D2 slide D1   G2              G1        D2 slide D1  slide   D2          D1
00 00  | 0 00 00 00  | 0  0 00 000   | 0 00 00 00 0  ||
00 00  | 0 00 00 00  | 0  0 00 000   | 0 00 00 00 0· ||
911 911 | 10 1211 910 910 | 11 11 109 1198 | 7 97 89 119 8· ||
```

*End tune at ∅ during repeat.

# THE SWALLOWTAIL JIG

O.K. Now, with the dulcimer tuned to DD-A-D, the D Mixolydian, by making the correct chords we can play in an *Aeolian Mode* of E or Em. The *melody* is written out below the chords for a *Dorian Mode* of E, tuned AA-B-E or AA-E-B. Just the melody string is written out since the rest are played open.

I am sure you'll surprise your local fiddlers when you use these chords to accompany their leads the next time you play.
The chords:

| | Em= | D= | G= | Em1= | D1= | G1= | D2= | G2= | D3= |
|---|---|---|---|---|---|---|---|---|---|
| | 1 | 0 | 0 | 5 | 0 | 7 | 4 | 3 | 0 |
| | 1 | 0 | 1 | 4 | 3 | 6 | 3 | 3 | 0 |
| | 1 | 2 | 3 | 3 | 4 | 5 | 2 | 3 | 0 |

Traditional
Arranged by Neal and Sally Hellman

Mixolydian tuning:

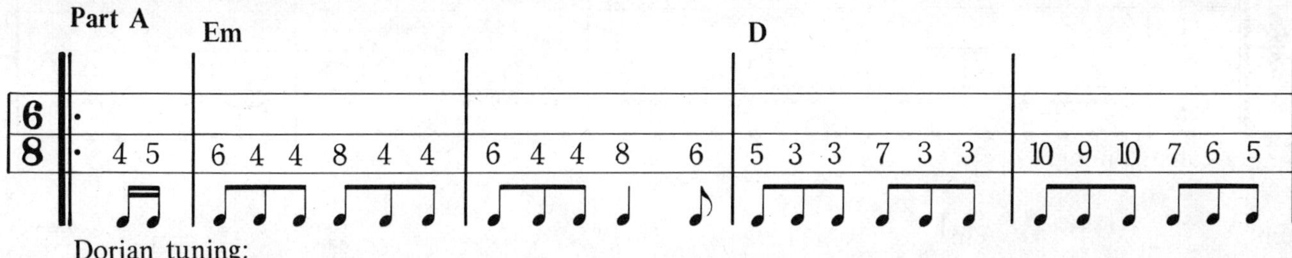


Dorian tuning:

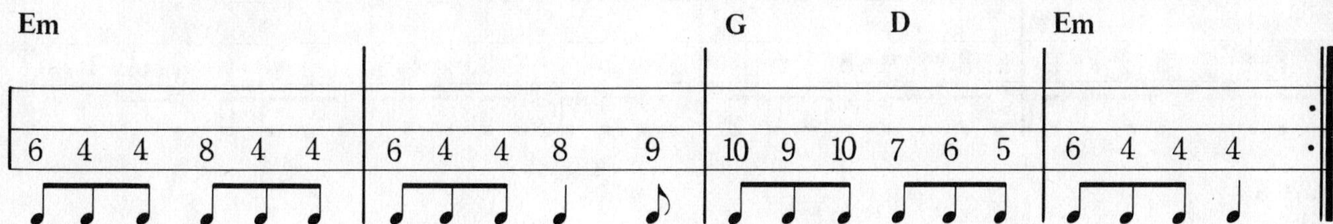


Part B

Em | Em1 | | D1 |

8 8 | 8 9 10 11 12 | 11 12 11 10 8 8 | 8 9 10 11 12 | 11 10 8 7 8 8

Em1 | | G1 D2 | G2 D3 Em

8 9 10 11 12 | 11 12 11 10 8 | 10 9 10 7 6 5 | 6 4 3 4

## TARBOLTON LODGE

The back-up chords here are another example of playing in a different mode (E Aeolian or Em) while tuned to Mixolydian (DD-A-D). The melody part, however, is written out for Aeolian tuning (DD-B-E). Since the top two strings are played open, only the melody is written out. Try playing the chords from underneath like a guitar (Position no. 3).

| | Em | D | Em1 | D1 | G |
|---|---|---|---|---|---|
| | 1 | 2 | 5 | 0 | 3 |
| = | 1 | 0 | 4 | 3 | 1 |
| | 1 | 0 | 3 | 4 | 0 |

Traditional
Arranged by Neal and Sally Hellman

Mixolydian tuning:

**Part A**

Em | D
4/4 |: 2 | 1 8 8 7 8 5 4 | 3 5 4 2 3 1 1 2 | 0 7 7 6½ 7 4 2 | 3 5 4 3 2 0 0 2 |

Aeolian tuning:

Em1 D1 | Em1 | G D | G D Em
| 1 8 8 7 8 9 10 11 | 9 8 7 9 8 5 5 4 | 3 4 5 3 2 3 4 2 | 5 3 4 2 3 1 1 :|

**Part B**

Em1 | D1
|: 9 | 10 9 8 9 10 8 12 8 | 10 8 12 8 10 8 8 9 | 7 8 9 10 11 7 9 7 | 4 5 4 3 2 0 0 2 |

Em1 D1 | Em1 | G D | G D Em
| 3 5 3 2 4 2 | 1 8 8 9 10 8 9 7 | 5 6½ 7 5 4 3 2 4 | 5 3 4 2 3 1 1 :|

## THE BLACK NAG

This English jig is in E Aeolian (Em); back-up chords are played in DD-A-D tuning, as usual, and the melody verison (tab) is in standard E Aeolian tuning (DD-B-E).

The melody is a little tricky to play fast, but it sounds beautiful when mastered.

| D= | Em[1]= | D[1]= | G[1]= | D[2]= | G[2]= | Bm= | Em[2]= |
|---|---|---|---|---|---|---|---|
| 0 | 1 | 0 | 3 | 0 | 3 | 5 | 5 |
| 0 | 1 | 0 | 3 | 0 | 3 | 5 | 4 |
| 0 | 1 | 2 | 3 | 4 | 5 | 0 | 3 |

Traditional
Arranged by Neal and Sally Hellman

Mixolydian tuning:

**Part A**

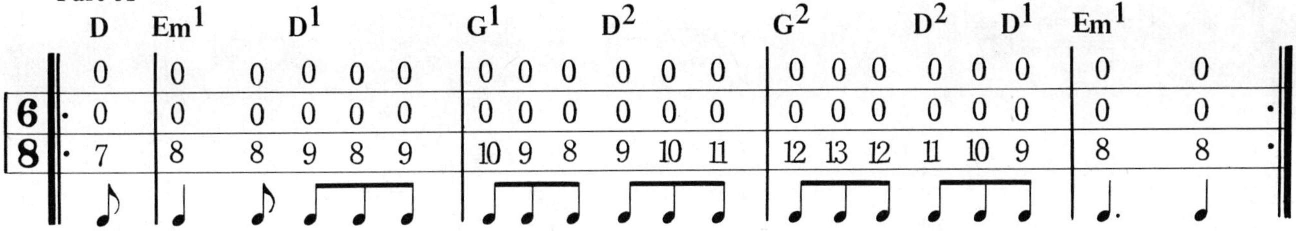

6/8

| | D | Em[1] D[1] | G[1] D[2] | G[2] D[2] D[1] | Em[1] |
|---|---|---|---|---|---|
| | 0 | 0 0 0 0 0 | 0 0 0 0 0 0 | 0 0 0 0 0 0 | 0 0 |
| | 0 | 0 0 0 0 0 | 0 0 0 0 0 0 | 0 0 0 0 0 0 | 0 0 |
| | 7 | 8 8 9 8 9 | 10 9 8 9 10 11 | 12 13 12 11 10 9 | 8 8 |

Aeolian tuning:

**Part B**

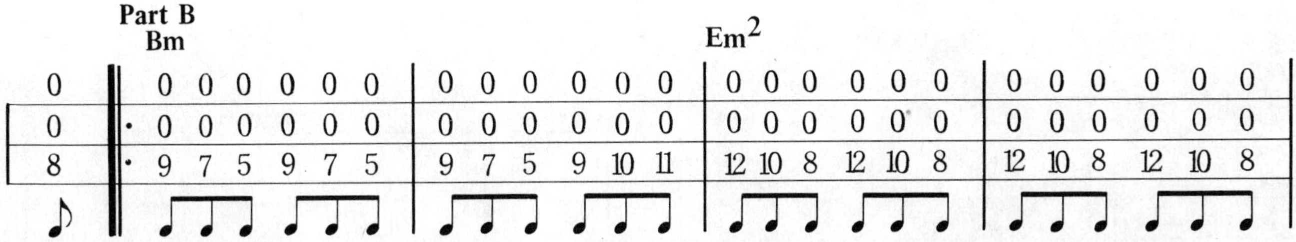

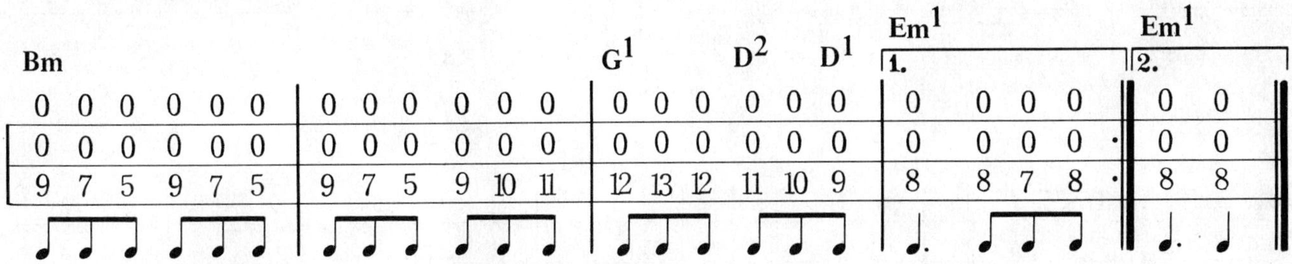

| | Bm | | Em[2] | |
|---|---|---|---|---|
| 0 | 0 0 0 0 0 0 | 0 0 0 0 0 0 | 0 0 0 0 0 0 | 0 0 0 0 0 0 |
| 0 | 0 0 0 0 0 0 | 0 0 0 0 0 0 | 0 0 0 0 0 0 | 0 0 0 0 0 0 |
| 8 | 9 7 5 9 7 5 | 9 7 5 9 10 11 | 12 10 8 12 10 8 | 12 10 8 12 10 8 |

| Bm | | G[1] D[2] D[1] | Em[1] 1. | Em[1] 2. |
|---|---|---|---|---|
| 0 0 0 0 0 0 | 0 0 0 0 0 0 | 0 0 0 0 0 0 | 0 0 0 0 | 0 0 |
| 0 0 0 0 0 0 | 0 0 0 0 0 0 | 0 0 0 0 0 0 | 0 0 0 0 | 0 0 |
| 9 7 5 9 7 5 | 9 7 5 9 10 11 | 12 13 12 11 10 9 | 8 8 7 8 | 8 8 |



*Note:* This tune is traditionally done in Dm, rather than Em. So if you want to keep with tradition, tune down one step: CC-G-C for the chords (Mixolydian C), and CC-A-D for the Aeolian. Chord positions would remain the same, although the names of the chords would be one step lower.

## PLANXTY IRWIN

Here is an example of playing in an Ionian Mode of G while tuned to the D Mixolydian, DD-A-D. This tune was composed by Turlough O'Carolan in the beginning of the 18th century. O'Carolan was a blind Irish harpist who composed over 2,000 beautiful pieces: "Carolan's Concerto," "Si Bhag Si More" and "Meagan Morgan" are some of his more popular pieces.

By Turlough O'Carolan
Arranged for dulcimer by Michael Hubbert and Michael Rugg

**Part A**

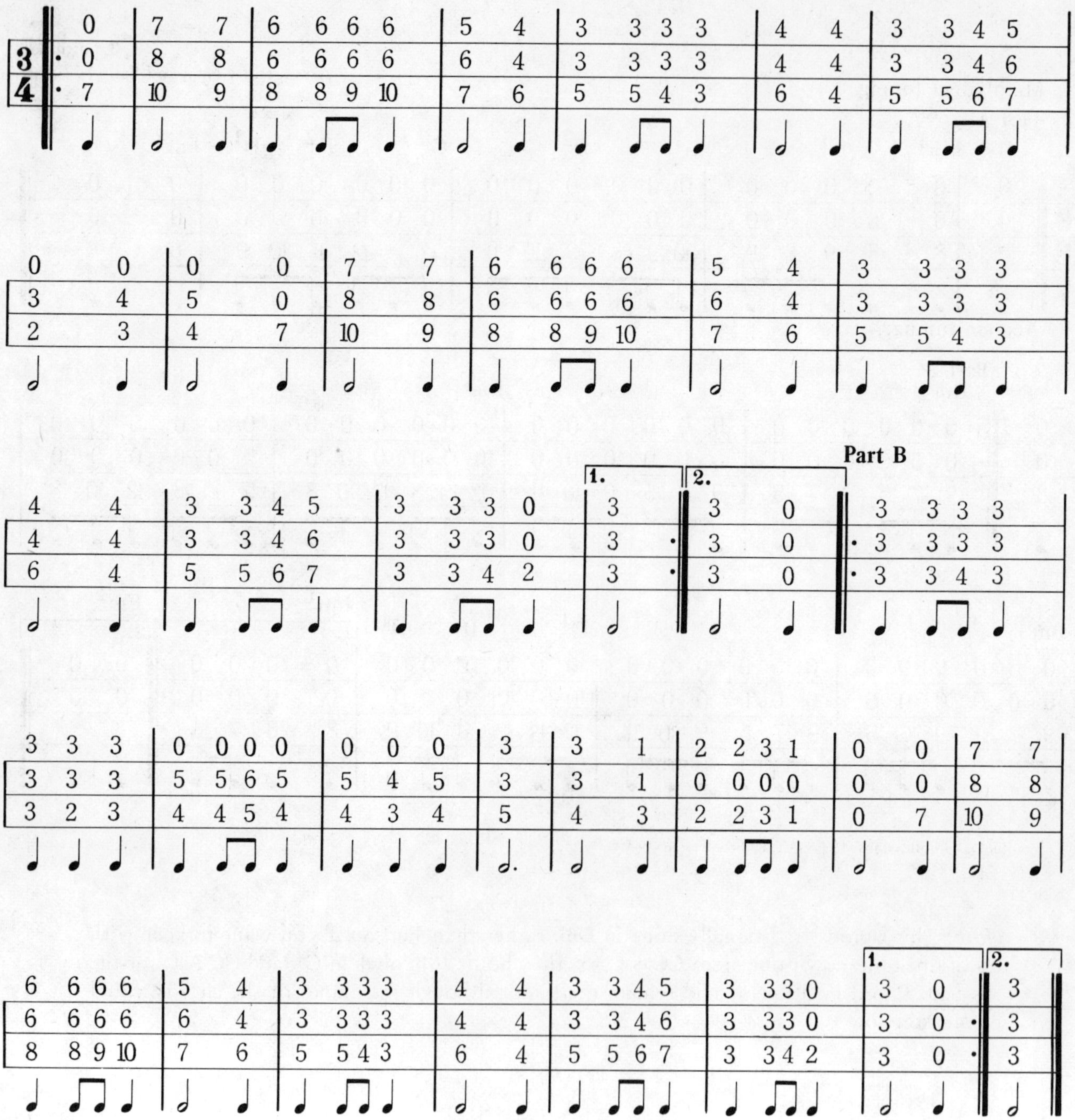

3/4
| 0 | 7 7 | 6 6 6 6 | 5 4 | 3 3 3 3 | 4 4 | 3 3 4 5 |
| 0 | 8 8 | 6 6 6 6 | 6 4 | 3 3 3 3 | 4 4 | 3 3 4 6 |
| 7 | 10 9 | 8 8 9 10 | 7 6 | 5 5 4 3 | 6 4 | 5 5 6 7 |

| 0 0 | 0 0 | 7 7 | 6 6 6 6 | 5 4 | 3 3 3 3 |
| 3 4 | 5 0 | 8 8 | 6 6 6 6 | 6 4 | 3 3 3 3 |
| 2 3 | 4 7 | 10 9 | 8 8 9 10 | 7 6 | 5 5 4 3 |

1. 2. **Part B**

| 4 4 | 3 3 4 5 | 3 3 3 0 | 1. 3 | 2. 3 0 | 3 3 3 3 |
| 4 4 | 3 3 4 6 | 3 3 3 0 | 3 | 3 0 | 3 3 3 3 |
| 6 4 | 5 5 6 7 | 3 3 4 2 | 3 | 3 0 | 3 3 4 3 |

| 3 3 3 | 0 0 0 0 | 0 0 0 | 3 | 3 1 | 2 2 3 1 | 0 0 | 7 7 |
| 3 3 3 | 5 5 6 5 | 5 4 5 | 3 | 3 1 | 0 0 0 0 | 0 0 | 8 8 |
| 3 2 3 | 4 4 5 4 | 4 3 4 | 5 | 4 3 | 2 2 3 1 | 0 7 | 10 9 |

| 6 6 6 6 | 5 4 | 3 3 3 3 | 4 4 | 3 3 4 5 | 3 3 3 0 | 1. 3 0 | 2. 3 |
| 6 6 6 6 | 6 4 | 3 3 3 3 | 4 4 | 3 3 4 6 | 3 3 3 0 | 3 0 | 3 |
| 8 8 9 10 | 7 6 | 5 5 4 3 | 6 4 | 5 5 6 7 | 3 3 4 2 | 3 0 | 3 |

## MAGGIE IN THE WOOD

This traditional Irish tune is another example of playing in G Ionian while tuned to DD-A-D. Once you master the chord pattern in this tune you will be able to play many more tunes in G. Try "Blackberry Blossom" or "Temperance Reel"; they all go well in this tuning.

Traditional Irish Polka
Arranged for dulcimer by Michael Hubbert and Michael Rugg

**Part A**

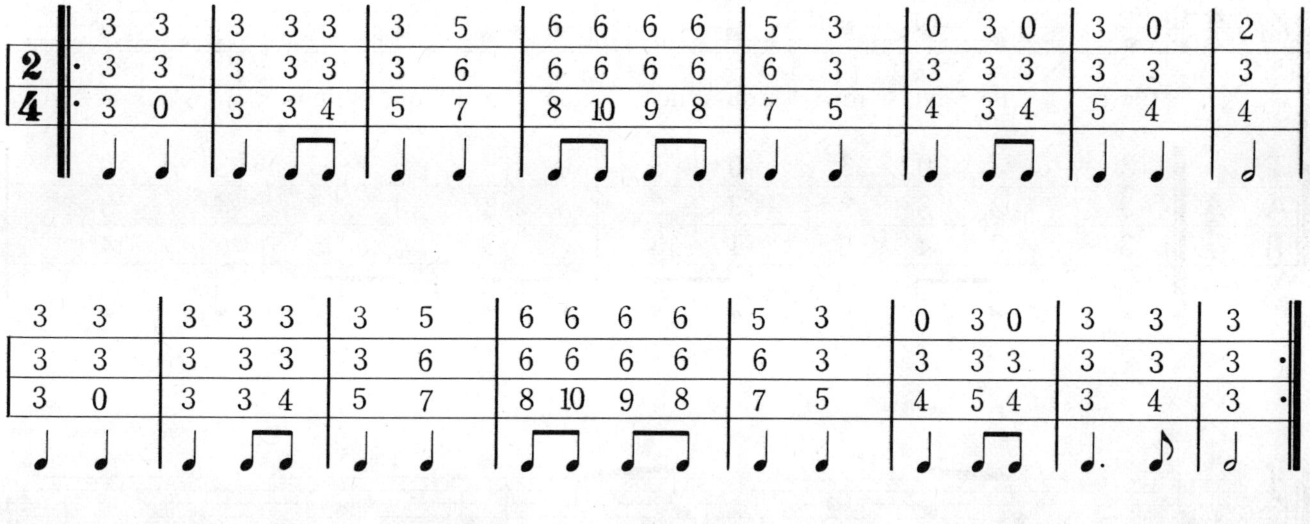

2/4

| 3 3 | 3 3 3 | 3 5 | 6 6 6 6 | 5 3 | 0 3 0 | 3 0 | 2 |
|---|---|---|---|---|---|---|---|
| 3 3 | 3 3 3 | 3 6 | 6 6 6 6 | 6 3 | 3 3 3 | 3 3 | 3 |
| 3 0 | 3 3 4 | 5 7 | 8 10 9 8 | 7 5 | 4 3 4 | 5 4 | 4 |

| 3 3 | 3 3 3 | 3 5 | 6 6 6 6 | 5 3 | 0 3 0 | 3 3 | 3 |
|---|---|---|---|---|---|---|---|
| 3 3 | 3 3 3 | 3 6 | 6 6 6 6 | 6 3 | 3 3 3 | 3 3 | 3 |
| 3 0 | 3 3 4 | 5 7 | 8 10 9 8 | 7 5 | 4 5 4 | 3 4 | 3 |

**Part B**

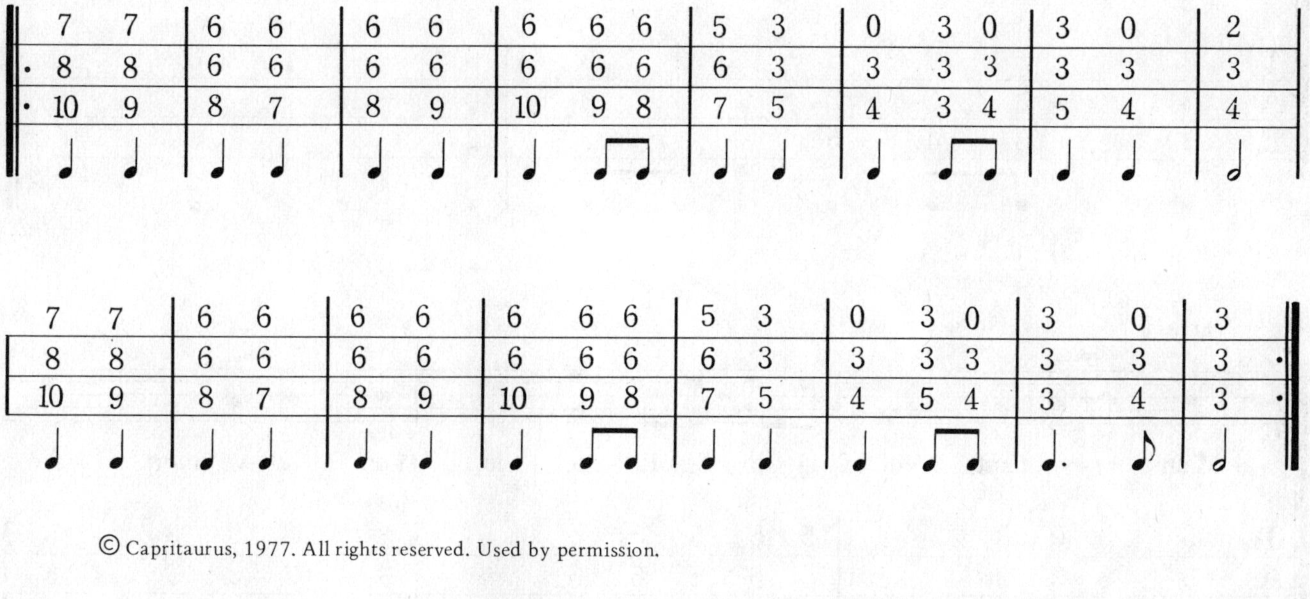

| 7 7 | 6 6 | 6 6 | 6 6 6 | 5 3 | 0 3 0 | 3 0 | 2 |
|---|---|---|---|---|---|---|---|
| 8 8 | 6 6 | 6 6 | 6 6 6 | 6 3 | 3 3 3 | 3 3 | 3 |
| 10 9 | 8 7 | 8 9 | 10 9 8 | 7 5 | 4 3 4 | 5 4 | 4 |

| 7 7 | 6 6 | 6 6 | 6 6 6 | 5 3 | 0 3 0 | 3 0 | 3 |
|---|---|---|---|---|---|---|---|
| 8 8 | 6 6 | 6 6 | 6 6 6 | 6 3 | 3 3 3 | 3 3 | 3 |
| 10 9 | 8 7 | 8 9 | 10 9 8 | 7 5 | 4 5 4 | 3 4 | 3 |

# C'EST L'AVIRON QUI NOUS MENE EN HAUT

(It is the Oar that Impels Us On)

This French Canadian tune is another example of playing in the Ionian Mode of G while tuned to the D Mixolydian (DD-A-D).

Traditional
Arranged by Neal and Sally Hellman

**Chorus:**

C'est l'a - vi - ron qui nous me - ne, qui nous me - ne,

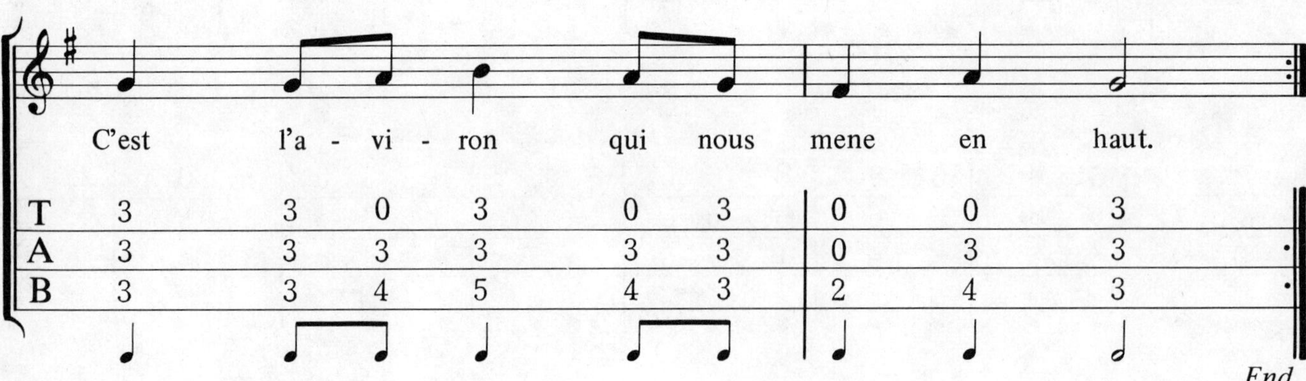


**Verse 1**

J'ai rencontré trois jolies demoiselles *(twice)*
J'ai point choisi, mais j'ai pris la plus belle.

**Chorus:**

C'est l'aviron qui nous mene, qui nous mene,
C'est l'aviron qui nous mene en haut.

J'ai point choisi, mais j'ai pris la plus belle; *(2x)*
J'l'y fis monter derrière, moi, sur ma selle.

**Chorus:**

C'est l'aviron . . .

J'l'y fis monter derrière, moi, sur ma selle; *(2x)*
J'y fis cent lieves sans parler avec elle.

**Chorus:**

J'y fis cent lieves sans parler avec elle; *(2x)*
Au bout des cent lieves, elle me d'mandit à boire.

**Chorus:**

Au bout des cent lieves, elle me d'mandit à boire; *(2x)*
Je l'ai menée auprès d'une fontaine.

**Chorus:**

Je l'ai menée auprès d'une fontaine; *(2x)*
Quand ell' fut là ell' ne voulut point boire.

**Chorus:**

Quand ell' fut là ell' ne voulut point boire. *(2x)*
Je l'ai menée au logis de son père.

Je l'ai menée au logis de son père, *(2x)*
Quand ell' fut là ell' buvait à pleins verres.

**Chorus:**

Quand ell' fut là ell' buvait à pleins verres, *(2x)*
À la santé de son père et sa mère.

**Chorus:**

À la santé de son père et sa mère, *(2x)*
À la santé de ses soeurs et ses frères.

**Chorus:**

À la santé de ses soeurs et ses frères, *(2x)*
À la santé d'celui que son coeur aimer.

**Chorus:**

## THE MINSTREL BOY

Once again, an example of playing in the Ionian Mode of G while tuned to the Mixolydian Mode of D.

Traditional
Arranged by Neal and Sally Hellman

**Part A**

4/4

3 | 3 3 3 3 3 0 3 | 3 5 7 7 7 | 6 5 3 2 3 3 5 3 | 0 3

3 | 3 3 3 4 3 3 3 | 3 6 8 7 8 | 6 6 3 3 3 4 6 3 | 3 3

0 | 3 3 4 6 5 4 3 | 5 7 10 9 10 | 8 7 5 4 5 6 7 5 | 4 3

**Part B**

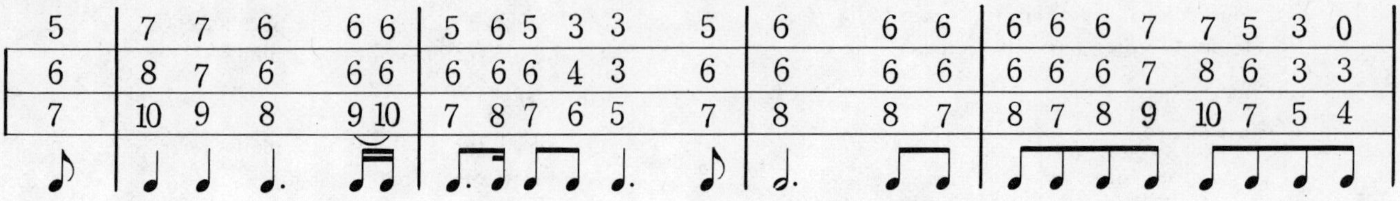

5 | 7 7 6 6 6 | 5 6 5 3 3 5 | 6 6 6 | 6 6 6 7 7 5 3 0

6 | 8 7 6 6 6 | 6 6 6 4 3 6 | 6 6 6 | 6 6 6 7 8 6 3 3

7 | 10 9 8 9 10 | 7 8 7 6 5 7 | 8 8 7 | 8 7 8 9 10 7 5 4

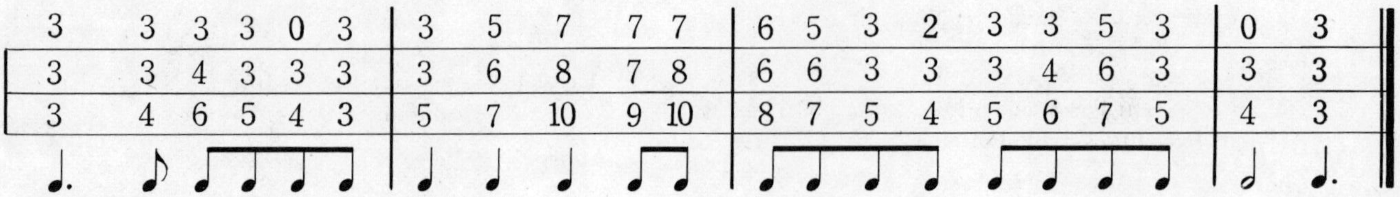

3 3 3 3 0 3 | 3 5 7 7 7 | 6 5 3 2 3 3 5 3 | 0 3

3 3 4 3 3 3 | 3 6 8 7 8 | 6 6 3 3 3 4 6 3 | 3 3

3 4 6 5 4 3 | 5 7 10 9 10 | 8 7 5 4 5 6 7 5 | 4 3

## THE FOREST OF GARTH

Tune your dulcimer to standard Mixolydian tuning (DD-A-D). By making the following chords, you will be playing this Irish step-dance in the A Dorian Mode.

Traditional
Arranged by Neal and Sally Hellman

**Part A**

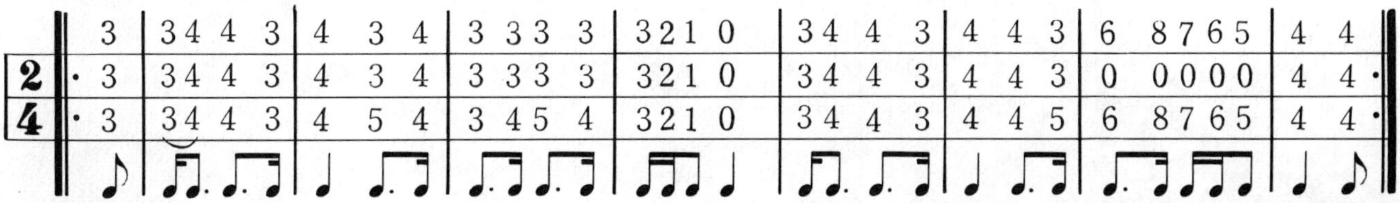

2/4

| | | | | | | | | |
|---|---|---|---|---|---|---|---|---|
| 3 | 34 4 3 | 4 3 4 | 3 33 3 | 321 0 | 34 4 3 | 4 4 3 | 6 8765 | 4 4 |
| 3 | 34 4 3 | 4 3 4 | 3 33 3 | 321 0 | 34 4 3 | 4 4 3 | 0 0000 | 4 4 |
| 3 | 34 4 3 | 4 5 4 | 3 45 4 | 321 0 | 34 4 3 | 4 4 5 | 6 8765 | 4 4 |

**Part B**

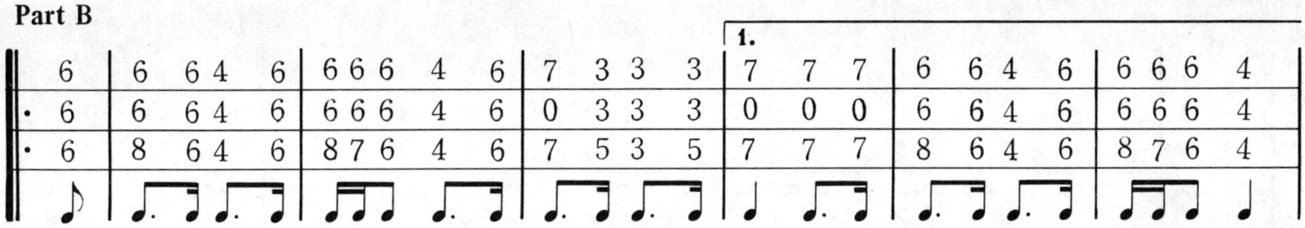

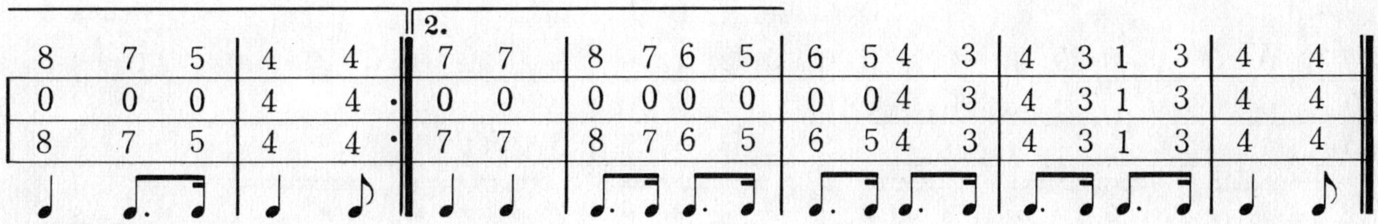

| | | | | 1. | | | | | 2. | | | | |
|---|---|---|---|---|---|---|---|---|---|---|---|---|---|
| 6 | 6 64 6 | 666 4 6 | 7 33 3 | 7 7 7 | 6 64 6 | 666 4 | 8 7 5 | 4 4 | 7 7 | 8 76 5 | 6 54 3 | 4 31 3 | 4 4 |
| 6 | 6 64 6 | 666 4 6 | 0 33 3 | 0 0 0 | 6 64 6 | 666 4 | 0 0 0 | 4 4 | 0 0 | 0 00 0 | 0 04 3 | 4 31 3 | 4 4 |
| 6 | 8 64 6 | 876 4 6 | 7 53 5 | 7 7 7 | 8 64 6 | 876 4 | 8 7 5 | 4 4 | 7 7 | 8 76 5 | 6 54 3 | 4 31 3 | 4 4 |

## BANK OF IRELAND

Here is another example of playing in a Dorian Mode of A (Am) while in the D Mixolydian tuning. Unlike the previous tune, here we play mostly back-up chords for the melody which is written below in the same mode (DD-A-D). In the "A" part it's mostly just a few chords behind the melody, but in the "B" part we come close to the melody in parts. Please don't get flustered by all the different "D" chords—they are all quite easy.

```
       4        0         1        7        9        8        5        11          1        0
Am =   4   D =  0   Em =  1  D1 =  0  D2 =  0  A =   0  D3 =  0  D4 =  0   Am1 =   0  D5 =  3
       4        0         1        7        9        8        5        11          4        4
```

Traditional
Arranged by Neal and Sally Hellman

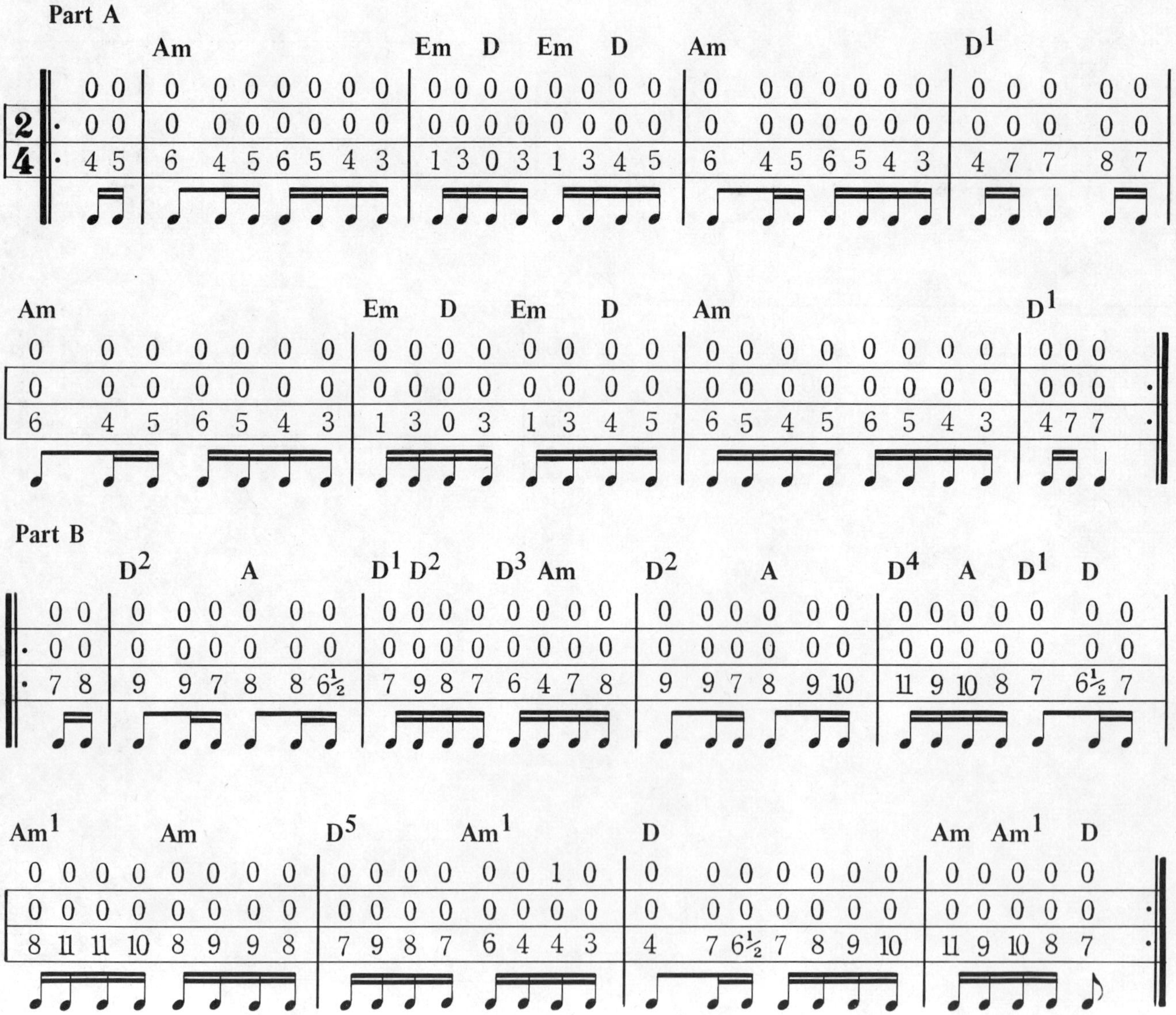

**Part A**

```
         Am                 Em  D  Em  D        Am                 D1
||  0 0 | 0  0 0 0 0 0 0 | 0 0 0 0 0 0 0 0 | 0  0 0 0 0 0 0 | 0 0 0  0 0 |
2|· 0 0 | 0  0 0 0 0 0 0 | 0 0 0 0 0 0 0 0 | 0  0 0 0 0 0 0 | 0 0 0  0 0 |
4|· 4 5 | 6  4 5 6 5 4 3 | 1 3 0 3 1 3 4 5 | 6  4 5 6 5 4 3 | 4 7 7  8 7 |
```

```
Am                  Em  D  Em  D        Am                  D1
0  0 0 0 0 0 0 | 0 0 0 0 0 0 0 0 | 0 0 0 0 0 0 0 0 | 0 0 0  ||
0  0 0 0 0 0 0 | 0 0 0 0 0 0 0 0 | 0 0 0 0 0 0 0 0 | 0 0 0 ·||
6  4 5 6 5 4 3 | 1 3 0 3 1 3 4 5 | 6 5 4 5 6 5 4 3 | 4 7 7 ·||
```

**Part B**

```
      D2        A        D1 D2   D3 Am       D2       A        D4    A   D1  D
||   0 0 | 0  0 0 0  0 0  | 0 0 0 0 0 0 0 0 | 0  0 0 0  0 0 | 0  0  0  0 0   0  0 |
||·  0 0 | 0  0 0 0  0 0  | 0 0 0 0 0 0 0 0 | 0  0 0 0  0 0 | 0  0  0  0 0   0  0 |
||·  7 8 | 9  9 7 8  8 6½ | 7 9 8 7 6 4 7 8 | 9  9 7 8  9 10| 11 9 10  8 7  6½  7 |
```

```
Am1         Am         D5          Am1       D                       Am Am1  D
0 0  0  0  0 0 0 0 | 0 0 0 0 0 0 1 0 | 0  0  0  0 0 0 0 0  | 0  0 0  0 0  ||
0 0  0  0  0 0 0 0 | 0 0 0 0 0 0 0 0 | 0  0  0  0 0 0 0 0  | 0  0 0  0 0 ·||
8 11 11 10 8 9 9 8 | 7 9 8 7 6 4 4 3 | 4  7  6½ 7 8 9 10   | 11 9 10 8 7 ·||
```

## TATER PATCH

Played in A modal while in the DD-A-D tuning. This is a good example of playing chords and melody in A while tuned in D Mixolydian. Sounds like a mad run through an open field under a full moon. The B Part is sometimes played 3 times.

Traditional
In the style of Teddy McKnight

**Part A**

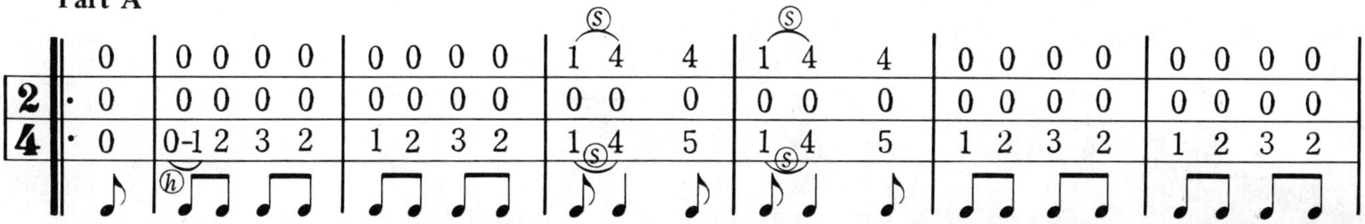

```
         S          S
|| 0 | 0 0 0 0 | 0 0 0 0 | 1 4   4 | 1 4   4 | 0 0 0 0 | 0 0 0 0 |
2|:0 | 0 0 0 0 | 0 0 0 0 | 0 0   0 | 0 0   0 | 0 0 0 0 | 0 0 0 0 |
4|:0 | 0-1 2 3 2 | 1 2 3 2 | 1 4  5 | 1 4   5 | 1 2 3 2 | 1 2 3 2 |
       h              S         S
```

**Part B**

```
8   7 5 | 4   :||: 3 | 3 3 3 3 | 3 3 3 3 | 8   8 | 3 4  ||
0   0 0 | 0   :||: 3 | 3 3 3 3 | 3 3 3 3 | 0   0 | 0 0 :||
8   7 5 | 4   :||: 3 | 5 3 4 3 | 5 3 4 3 | 8   9 | 3 4 :||
```

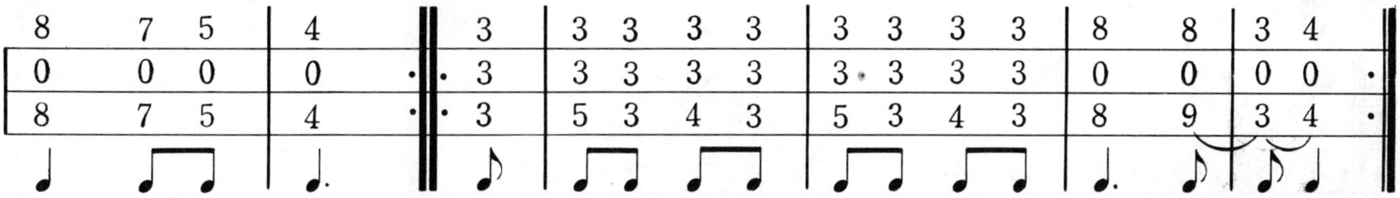

# DEVIL'S DREAM

Here is another example of how you can play in the key of A while in the DD-A-D (key of D) tuning, not for the melody but for the back-up chords: A, Bm and E. Once again the melody is written below the chords so you know how the tune goes, for the Mixolydian tuning of A: AA-A-E or AA-E-A, or however you tune to A.

As before, I prefer just the chord version, because fiddlers play so fast it's almost impossible to keep up with the melody. Once you've learned this, you'll also know "The Mason's Apron" and more tunes which have a similar chord structure.

```
      4          1           5           2        1
A1 =  0   A2 =   0   Bm1 =   5   Bm2 =   1   E =  1
      4          1           0           0        1
```

Traditional
Arranged by
Neal and Sally Hellman and Rick Scott

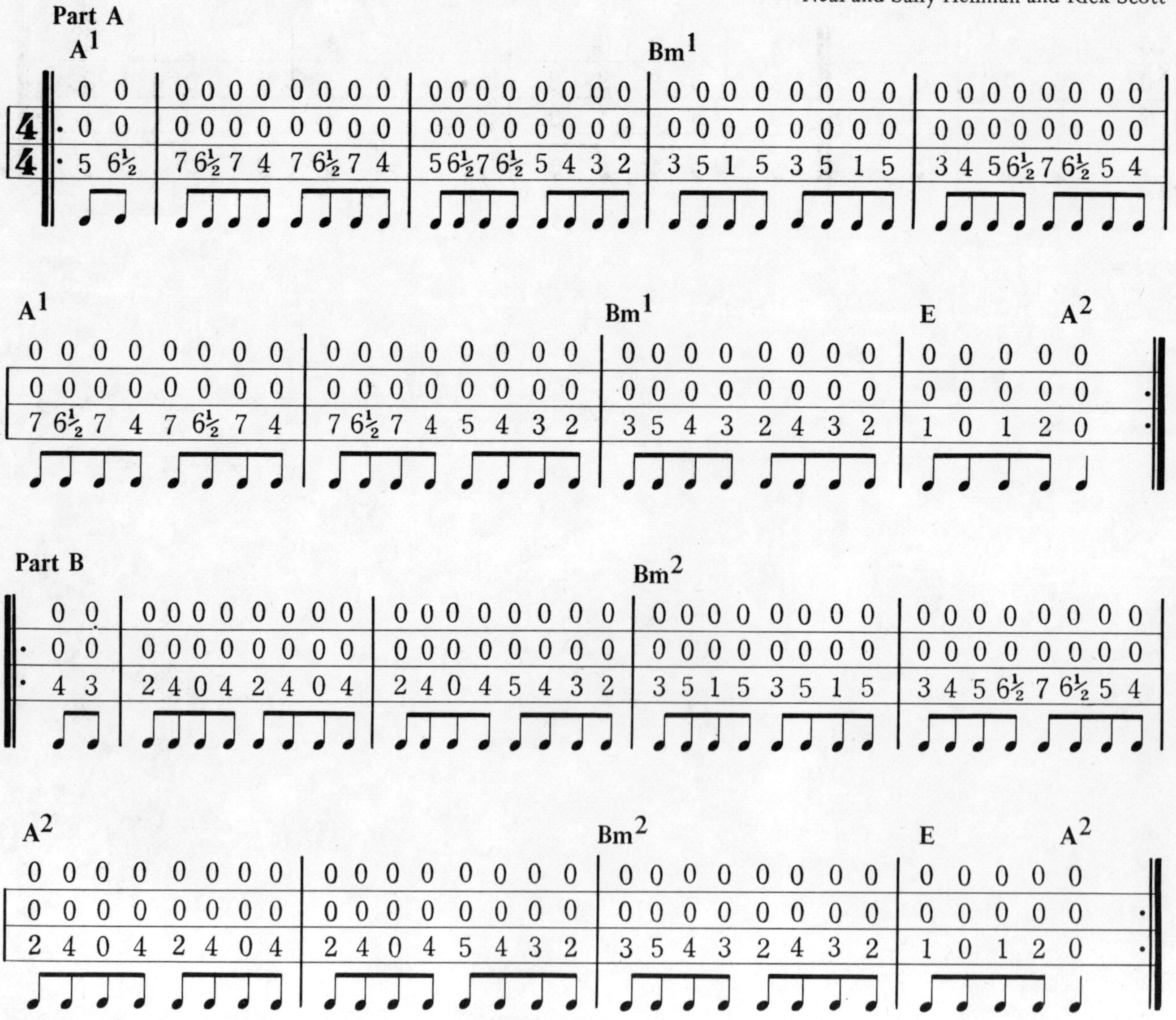

**Part A**

```
     A1                                                   Bm1
4 ||: 0 0    | 0 0 0 0 0 0 0 0 | 0 0 0 0 0 0 0 0       | 0 0 0 0 0 0 0 0 | 0 0 0 0 0 0 0 0       |
  ||: 0 0    | 0 0 0 0 0 0 0 0 | 0 0 0 0 0 0 0 0       | 0 0 0 0 0 0 0 0 | 0 0 0 0 0 0 0 0       |
4 ||: 5 6½   | 7 6½ 7 4 7 6½ 7 4 | 5 6½ 7 6½ 5 4 3 2   | 3 5 1 5 3 5 1 5 | 3 4 5 6½ 7 6½ 5 4     |
```

```
A1                                        Bm1                E          A2
0 0 0 0 0 0 0 0     | 0 0 0 0 0 0 0 0     | 0 0 0 0 0 0 0 0 | 0 0 0 0 0    :||
0 0 0 0 0 0 0 0     | 0 0 0 0 0 0 0 0     | 0 0 0 0 0 0 0 0 | 0 0 0 0 0    :||
7 6½ 7 4 7 6½ 7 4   | 7 6½ 7 4 5 4 3 2    | 3 5 4 3 2 4 3 2 | 1 0 1 2 0    :||
```

**Part B**

```
                                                   Bm2
||: 0 0 | 0 0 0 0 0 0 0 0 | 0 0 0 0 0 0 0 0 | 0 0 0 0 0 0 0 0 | 0 0 0 0 0 0 0 0       |
||: 0 0 | 0 0 0 0 0 0 0 0 | 0 0 0 0 0 0 0 0 | 0 0 0 0 0 0 0 0 | 0 0 0 0 0 0 0 0       |
||: 4 3 | 2 4 0 4 2 4 0 4 | 2 4 0 4 5 4 3 2 | 3 5 1 5 3 5 1 5 | 3 4 5 6½ 7 6½ 5 4     |
```

```
A2                                    Bm2                E          A2
0 0 0 0 0 0 0 0 | 0 0 0 0 0 0 0 0 | 0 0 0 0 0 0 0 0 | 0 0 0 0 0    :||
0 0 0 0 0 0 0 0 | 0 0 0 0 0 0 0 0 | 0 0 0 0 0 0 0 0 | 0 0 0 0 0    :||
2 4 0 4 2 4 0 4 | 2 4 0 4 5 4 3 2 | 3 5 4 3 2 4 3 2 | 1 0 1 2 0    :||
```

## SEA WIND

Here is an example of playing in the key of Bm while tuned to D Mixolydian (DD-A-D). Here are some new chords:

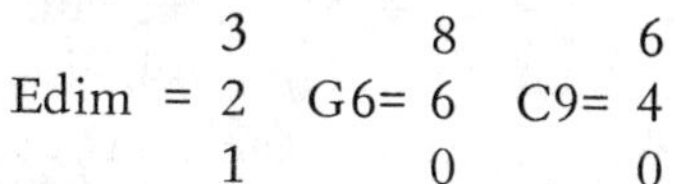


Words and music
by Daniel S. Rubin

Verse:

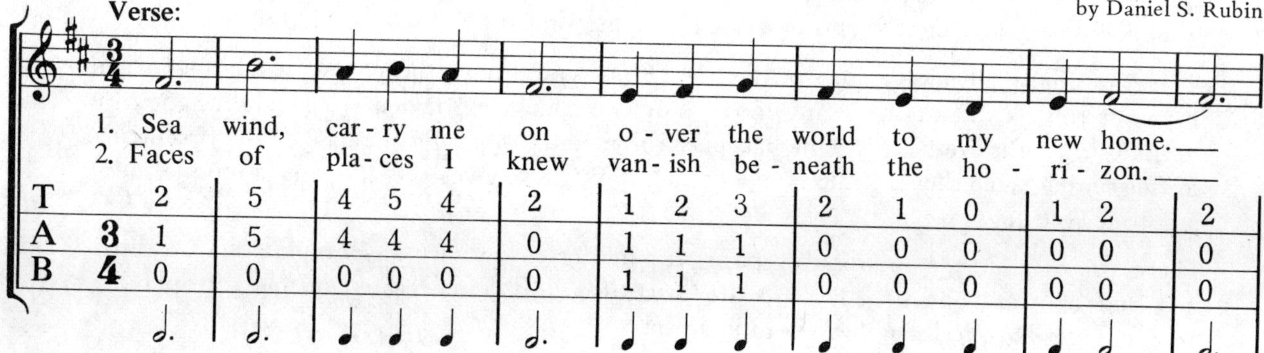


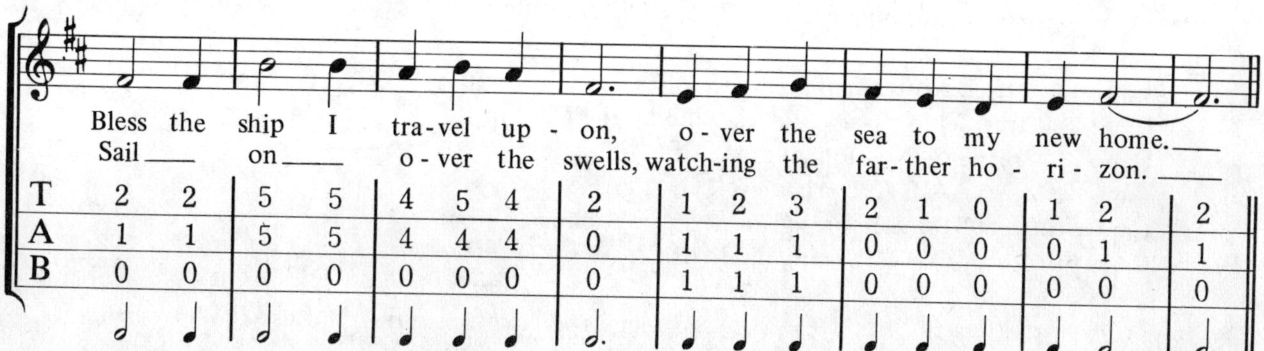


Chorus:

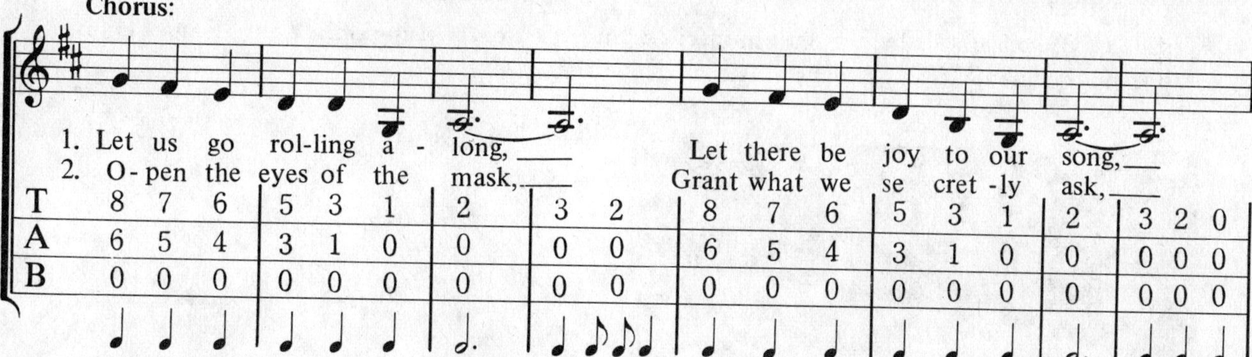


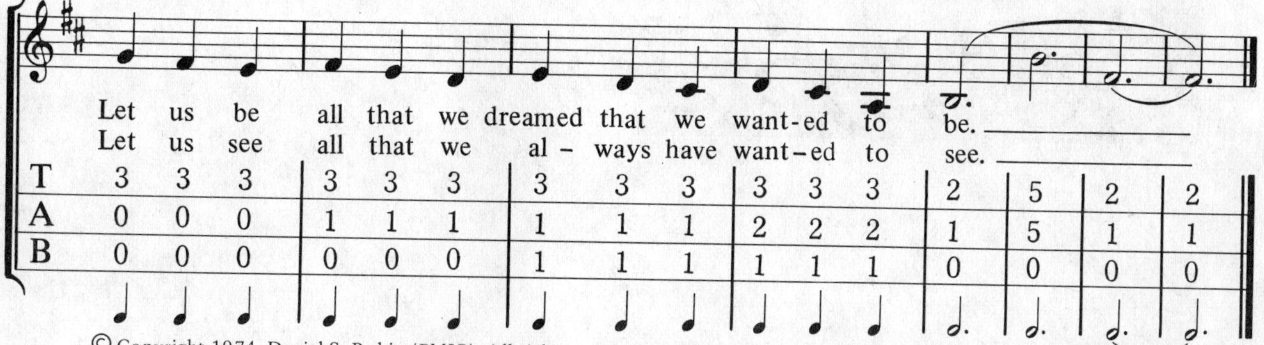




*Repeat first verse*

# Changing Modes by Using a Capo

By using a simple homemade capo we can play in all the modes, and in seven different keys, without retuning the strings. We will use the standard D Mixolydian tuning (DD-A-D) once again as our example, although this technique can be done in any standard Mixolydian mode.

Find yourself a very thick rubber band and a chopstick that has flat sides. Place the chopsticks across the neck to the left of any fret you desire. Put the rubber band around the long end of the stick, and then gently wrap it underneath the dulcimer and around the short end of the chopstick. If it is too loose, you might have to double the rubber band or use a smaller one. You'll know when it's right by the clear sound that the dulcimer will produce.

There are many advantages to this method. First, you'll have the power of the open strum for your tonic or key note in any mode. You can change mode and key by sliding the capo up and down the fretboard. (One can play the melody on either the bass or the first strings in this tuning since they are the same note.) Capoing also gives the dulcimer a unique sound and tone-coloring.

There are, of course, some disadvantages. It's harder to do with an hourglass-shaped dulcimer than a "teardrop" one. It "cuts off" part of your dulcimer, thus limiting your playing. You will also have to learn new chord positions.

Here is a summary of capoing each fret in the DD-A-D tuning:

Capo 1st fret: EE-B-E, Aeolian mode of E (Em).
Capo 2nd fret: F♯ F♯-C♯-F♯, Locrian mode of F♯ (F♯m).
Capo 3rd fret: GG-D-G, Ionian mode of G (G Major).
Capo 4th fret: AA-E-A, Dorian mode of A (Am).
Capo 5th fret: BB-FE-B, Phrygian mode of B (Bm).
Capo 6th fret: CC-G-C, Lydian mode of C.

If you have the "extra" fret (6½) you can place the capo around it and use the bass string for the melody. We call this the "Pi-Allah-Mode."

*Note:* If you have a dulcimer with an arched fingerboard try using one of those small Dunlap capos available in any decent music supply store.

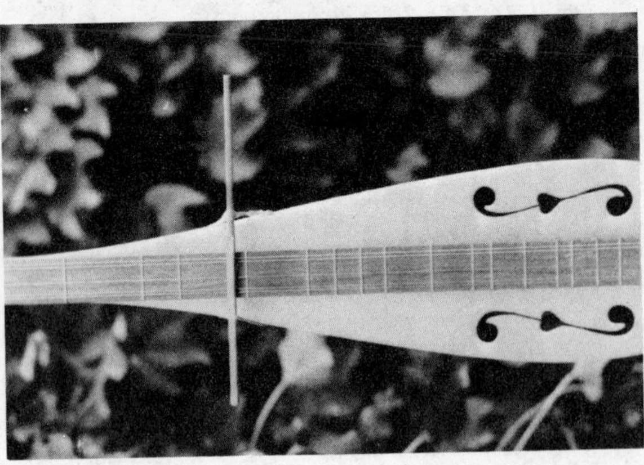

## RAIN AND SNOW

Place the capo to the left of the 1st fret. Your standard Mixolydian of D (DD-A-D) now becomes an Aeolian Mode of E (Em). One cannot make the same chords as in the standard Aeolian of E (DD-B-E) but chords are possible. Also, the scale starts on an open strum, not on the first fret. *Remember, we now count the frets from where our capo is, not from the nut.*

Traditional
Arranged by Neal and Sally Hellman

See her coming on down the stairs,
Combing back her long yellow hair,
And her cheeks were as red as the rose,
As the rose, as the rose,
And her cheeks were as red as the rose.

See you lying in the shade countin' every dime
I made
I'm so broke and I'm hungry too,
Hungry too, hungry too,
I'm so broke and I'm hungry too.

Well she came into the room
Where she met her fatal doom,
And I'm not gonna be treated this-a-way
This-a-way, this-a-way,
And I'm not gonna be treated this-a-way.

Oh I ain't got no use
For your red apple juice,
And I'm not gonna be treated this-a-way,
This-a-way, this-a-way
Saying I'm not gonna be treated this-a-way.

Oh, I married me a wife,
Give me trouble all my life,
Ran me out in the cold rain and snow.
Rain and snow, rain and snow,
Ran me out in the cold rain and snow.

# The Locrian Mode

Before starting, read about the Locrian mode again in the "Modes and Tunings" section. You know already that this mode's "unevenness" makes it very hard to compose in. Let us first explore this mode without using a capo. B♭ B♭ -A-D or AA-G♯ -C♯ are standard Locrian tunings. E♭ E♭ -G-D or DD-F♯ -C♯ are "new" Locrian tunings. (Consult the quick-tune chart (p. 8 ) for easy ways to get into the above tunings from other modes.) The scale starts on the 2nd fret and ends on the 9th fret. The 6½ or "extra" fret comes in very handy in this mode. Here are some chords written out for the standard Locrian mode (B B -A-D):

| | | | | | | | | | | | | | | | | | | | | |
|---|---|---|---|---|---|---|---|---|---|---|---|---|---|---|---|---|---|---|---|---|
| *Bass* | 0 | 4 | 3 | 3 | 0 | 4 | 3 | 2 | 4 | 5 | 7 | 3 | 0 | 4 | 7 | 6 | 7 | 7 | 7 | 7 | 6 |
| *Middle* | 3 | 3 | 0 | 3 | 3 | 3 | 3 | 2 | 4 | 5 | 7 | 3 | 3 | 3 | 6 | 6 | 6 | 7 | 7 | 6 | 8 |
| *Melody* | 2 | 2 | 2 | 2 | 4 | 5 | 5 | 6 | 6½ | 6½ | 6½ | 6½ | 6½ | 6½ | 7 | 8 | 8 | 8 | 9 | 9 | 9 |

You may chord the melody string(s) and bass at the same fret anywhere on the scale: 2/0/2 or 7/0/7, etc. A combination of chords and melody-string slides and hammer-ons can lead to some very powerful dulcimer playing.

### Capoing Into the Locrian Mode

OK, back to our standard Mixolydian of D (DD-A-D). Now, place your capo to the left of the second fret, and you're in a Locrian mode of F♯: F♯ F♯-C♯-F♯ (key of F♯m). Having the advantage of the open strum will really help you in this mode. If you're playing a lead way up in the high frets all you need to do is strum open to return to the tonic or key note. You can also play the melody on the bass string, which sounds very haunting in this mode.

To obtain a more "Eastern" effect take another chopstick and cut very small grooves where the strings will lie. This will make the strings "buzz," thus sounding similar to a sitar.

I feel that by now you have enough information to get started in this mode. As you can hear, this mode sounds very different from the ones we usually play in. It has a completely different color and vibration. I will leave it up to you to compose in this mode, but may I suggest the following: Instead of trying to fit a traditional-type tune in this mode, try using it to "break loose" and play what you feel inside your heart. It's excellent for an evening raga by candlelight. We all have conceptions of how a dulcimer should sound—this mode I'm sure will alter and expand those conceptions. Play on!

## SILLY BILL

Now we will play a tune in the G Ionian Mode while tuned to the D Mixolydian. Place the capo to the left of the 3rd fret and we will have a G chord when the strings are strummed open. Try this tune without the capo, using the chords from the chart; it sounds really happy and bright.

Traditional
In the style of Bonnie Russell

**Part A**

Capo: 3rd fret

2/4

| 00 | 00000000 | 0000 | 0 00 | 0 00 | 00000000 | 0000 | 0 00 | 0 |
|---|---|---|---|---|---|---|---|---|
| 00 | 00000000 | 0000 | 0 00 | 0 00 | 00000000 | 0000 | 0 00 | 0 |
| 21 | 01210123 | 4442 | 3 21 | 2 21 | 01210123 | 4442 | 3 21 | 0 |

**Part B**

| 2 | 3 3 | 33333 | 0 00 | 2 | 0 0 | 2 0 | 0 00 | 0 (end of repeat) | 0 (Final Ending) | 0000 | 0 |
|---|---|---|---|---|---|---|---|---|---|---|---|
| 0 | 3 3 | 33333 | 0 00 | 0 | 0 0 | 0 0 | 0 00 | 0 | 0 | 0000 | 0 |
| 4 | 5 3 | 54543 | 7 65 | 4 | 7 2 | 4 2 | 3 21 | 0 | 7 | 5421 | 0 |

Raymond Melton

## THE WELL BELOW THE VALLEY

Tune to the standard Mixolydian of D (DD-A-D) and place the capo to the left of the 4th fret. Now you have a Dorian Mode of A ("Am"). One can play almost any of the traditional minor-key tunes in this position. Remember, the capo becomes our new "nut" so count from the capo, not the nut. "Childe Ballade no. 21" ("The Maid and the Palmer") bears a strong resemblance to this Irish air. The woman is Mary Magdalen and the man Jesus. The woman has committed incest with her family. She had 6 children, and she murders them all. Jesus has promised to forgive her after she serves time in Hell. Compared to the Danish version this one is mild.

Traditional
In the style of Ruthie Dorenfeld

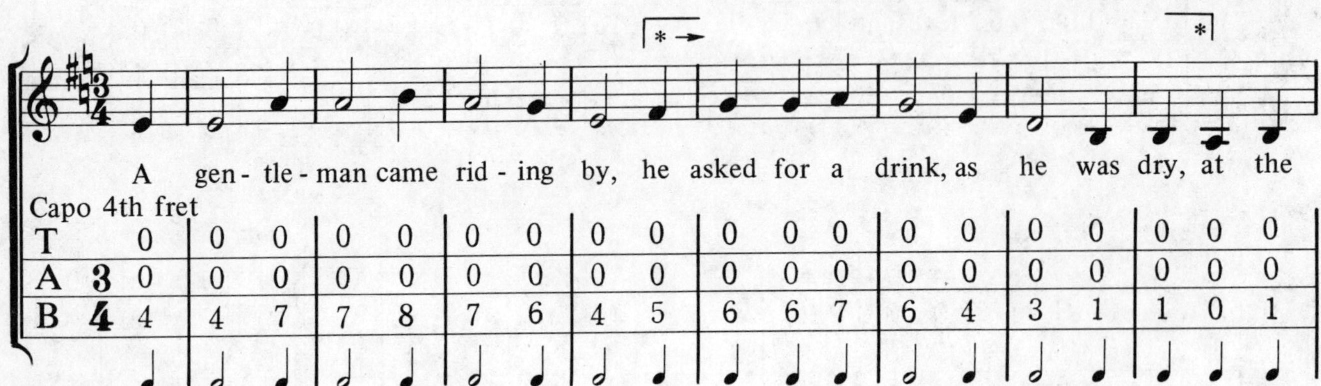


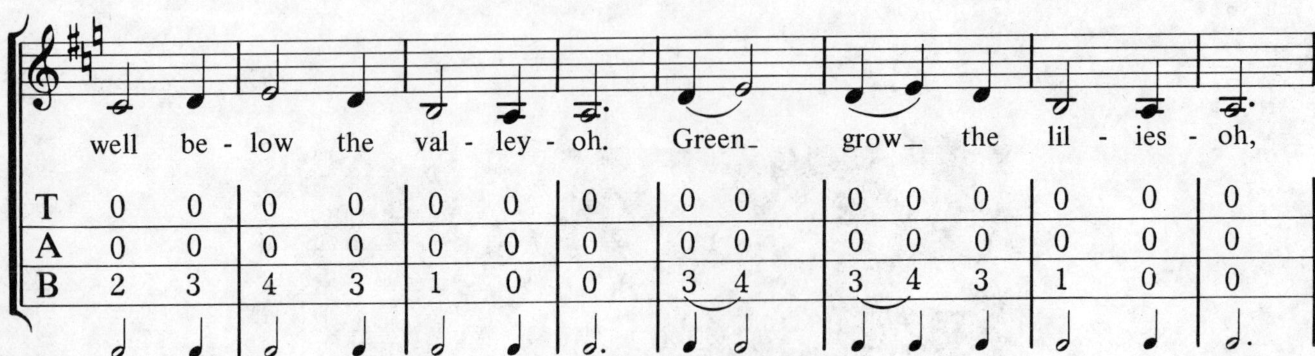


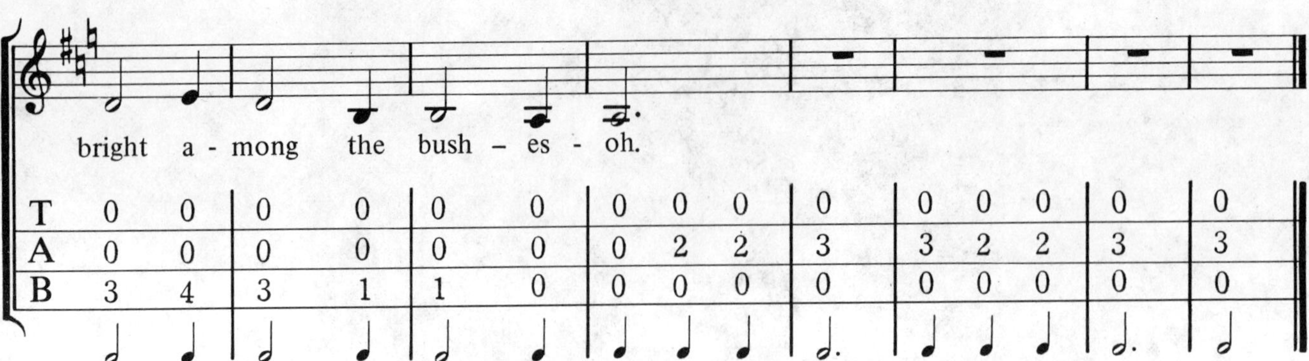


*Do not play between these lines, [* ——→ *], for verses 7, 8, 9, 11, 12, 13, 15, or 16.

The cup is full unto the brim,
If I were to stoop I might fall in,

Chorus:

At the well below the valley-oh,
Green grow the lilies-oh,
Bright among the bushes-oh.

If your true love was passing by
You'd give him a drink as he rode by,
Chorus:

She swore behind, she swore before,
That her true love had never been born,
Chorus:

As to him you've falsely sworn,
For six fine children you have born,
Chorus:

If you be a man of noble fame
You'll tell to me the father of them.
Chorus:

There's two of them by your uncle John,
Chorus:

Another by your brother Tom,
Chorus:

Another two by your father dear,
Chorus:

If you be a man of noble fame
You'd tell to me what happened to them.
Chorus:

There's two of them by the kitchen door,
Chorus:

Another two under the stable floor,
Chorus :

Another two beneath the well,
Chorus: *(omit the word "At")*

If you be a man of noble fame,
What will to meself be done?
Chorus:

There'll be seven years a' ringing the bell,
Chorus:

Another seven a' courtin' in Hell,
Chorus:

Seven years courtin' in Hell.
But the Lord will come to save your soul.
Chorus:

## BOATIN' UP SANDY

Capo on the 4th fret as you did for "The Well Below The Valley." I would definitely suggest using your fingers (index and middle) especially since you need to strike the middle string a few times.

Traditional
In the style of Molly Mearns

**Part A**
Capo 4th fret

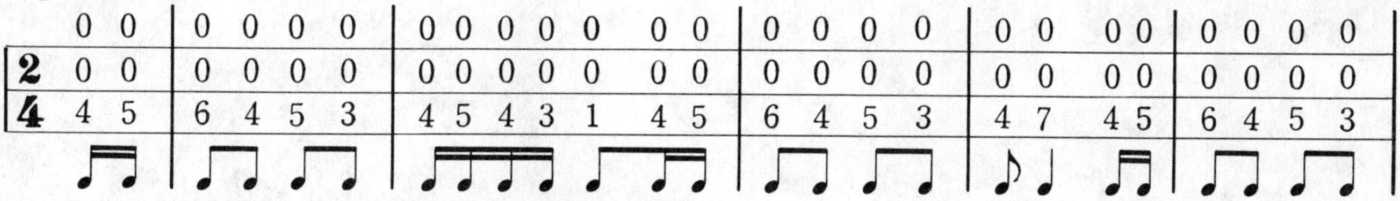

| | | | | | |
|---|---|---|---|---|---|
| 0 0 | 0 0 0 0 | 0 0 0 0 0 0 0 | 0 0 0 0 | 0 0 0 0 | 0 0 0 0 |
| **2** 0 0 | 0 0 0 0 | 0 0 0 0 0 0 0 | 0 0 0 0 | 0 0 0 0 | 0 0 0 0 |
| **4** 4 5 | 6 4 5 3 | 4 5 4 3 1 4 5 | 6 4 5 3 | 4 7 4 5 | 6 4 5 3 |

**Part B**

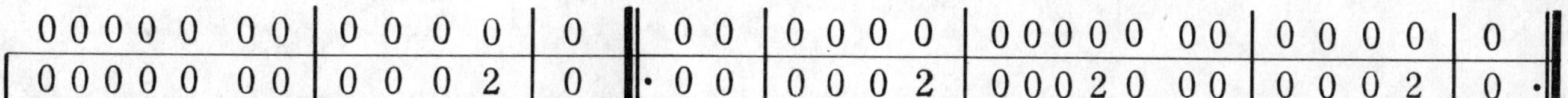

| | | | | | | | |
|---|---|---|---|---|---|---|---|
| 0 0 0 0 0 0 0 | 0 0 0 0 | 0 | 0 0 | 0 0 0 0 | 0 0 0 0 0 0 0 | 0 0 0 0 | 0 |
| 0 0 0 0 0 0 0 | 0 0 0 2 | 0 | · 0 0 | 0 0 0 2 | 0 0 0 2 0 0 0 | 0 0 0 2 | 0 · |
| 4 5 4 3 1 0 1 | 2 0 1 0 | 0 | · 0 1 | 2 0 1 0 | 0 1 0 0 0 0 1 | 2 0 1 0 | 0 · |

## CLUCK OLD HEN

Placing our capo to the left of the 4th fret gives us a Dorian Mode of A (Am).

Traditional
Arranged by Neal and Sally Hellman

4/4

| | Part A | | Part B | |
|---|---|---|---|---|
| String 1 | 0 0 0 0 0 | 0 0 0 0 0 0 0 | 0 0 0 0 | 0 0 0 0 0 0 |
| String 2 | 0 0 0 0 3 | 0 0 0 0 0 3 0 | 3 3 3 2 | 3 3 3 3 3 3 |
| String 3 | 4 7 6 4 3 | 4 7 6 4 4 2 0 | 0 2 0 0 | 0 2 3 4 2 0 |

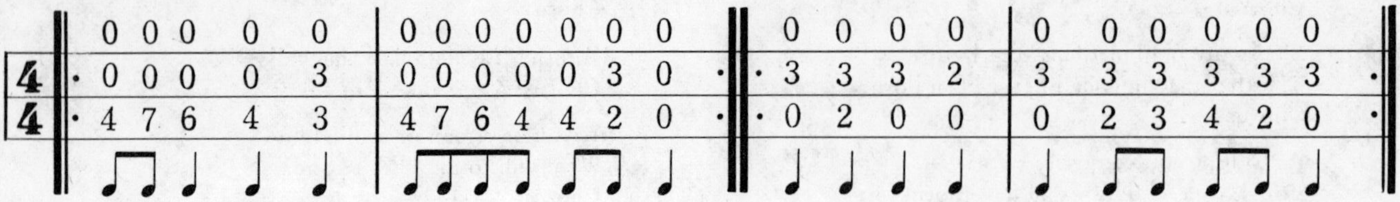

## JUNE APPLE

By utilizing the "extra" fret and making the correct chords one can play in the key of A Major while capoed at the 4th fret and tuned to DD-A-D. This of course means one can play any of the traditional tunes usually played in A: "Old Joe Clark," "Cherokee Shuffle," "Angeline," etc.

Traditional
Arranged by Neal and Sally Hellman

**Part A**
Capo 4th fret

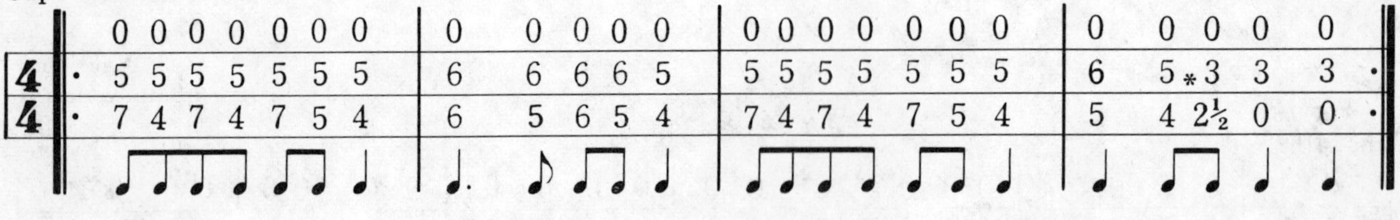

4/4

| | | | | |
|---|---|---|---|---|
| String 1 | 0 0 0 0 0 0 0 | 0 0 0 0 | 0 0 0 0 0 0 0 | 0 0 0 0 0 |
| String 2 | 5 5 5 5 5 5 5 | 6 6 6 6 5 | 5 5 5 5 5 5 5 | 6 5 * 3 3 3 |
| String 3 | 7 4 7 4 7 5 4 | 6 5 6 5 4 | 7 4 7 4 7 5 4 | 5 4 2½ 0 0 |

**Part B**

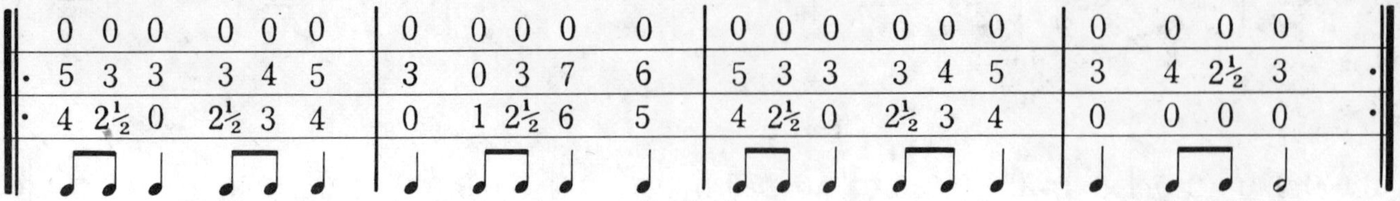

| | | | | |
|---|---|---|---|---|
| String 1 | 0 0 0 0 0 0 | 0 0 0 0 0 | 0 0 0 0 0 0 | 0 0 0 0 |
| String 2 | 5 3 3 3 4 5 | 3 0 3 7 6 | 5 3 3 3 4 5 | 3 4 2½ 3 |
| String 3 | 4 2½ 0 2½ 3 4 | 0 1 2½ 6 5 | 4 2½ 0 2½ 3 4 | 0 0 0 0 |



**The 6½ fret becomes "2½" when the dulcimer is capoed on the 4th fret.

## MARJORIE

By capoing on the 5th fret (tuning: DD-A-D) one will be playing and singing this song in an Phrygian Mode of B ("Bm"). If you do not have the "extra" fret, move the capo down to the 4th fret.

Traditional
Arranged by Bonnie Carol

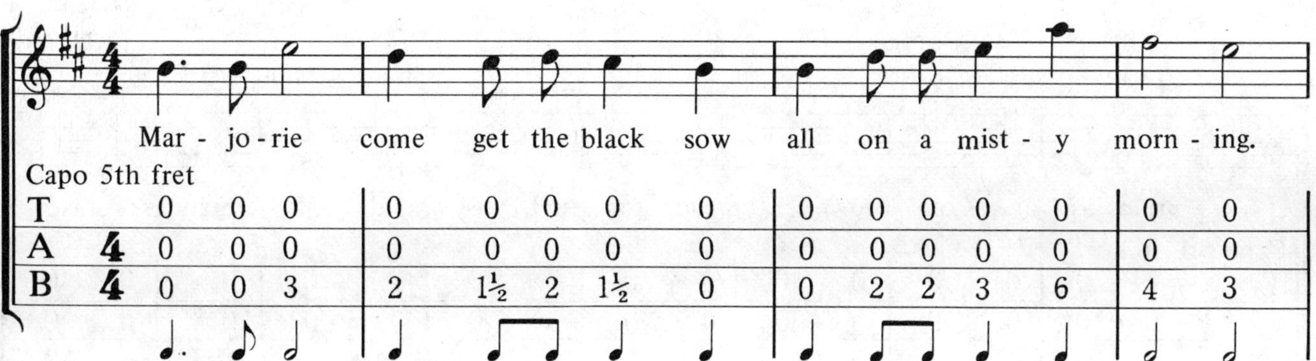

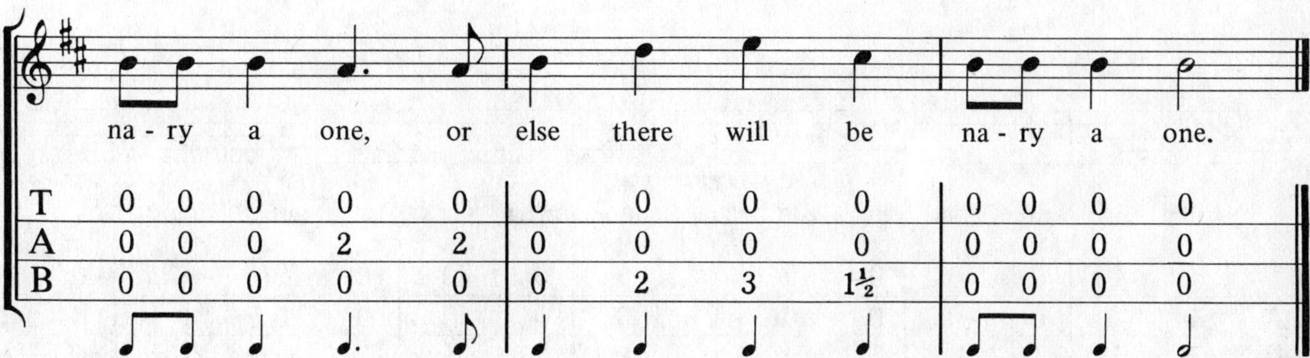

## BRING US IN GOOD ALE

Capoing on the 5th fret puts us in the Phrygian Mode. In the DD-A-D tuning, this would be a sort of Bm. This example will show the usefulness of the "extra" 6½ fret. (One can play the tune without it by utilizing the 4th fret of the middle string.) By using the 6½ fret we will actually be playing in the Dorian Mode. Since we count the frets from where the capo is our "extra" fret shall be called 1½ here.

Traditional
In the style of Timmy Hart

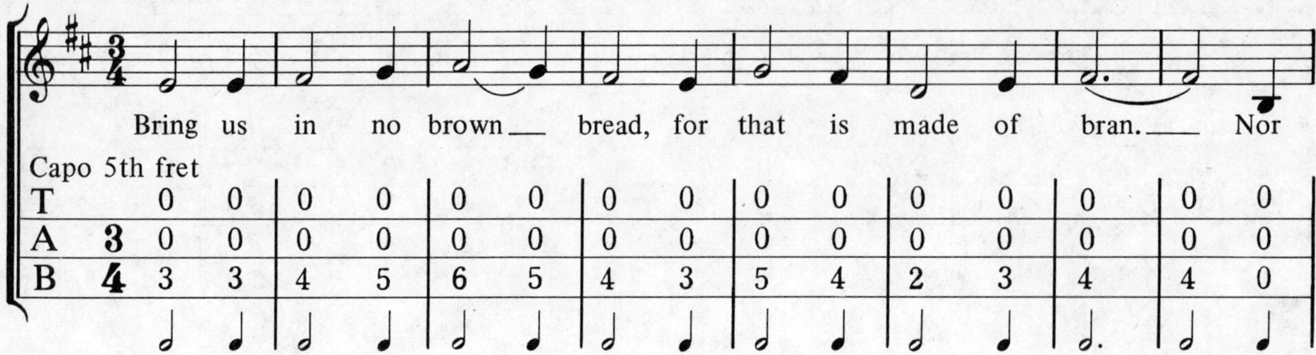


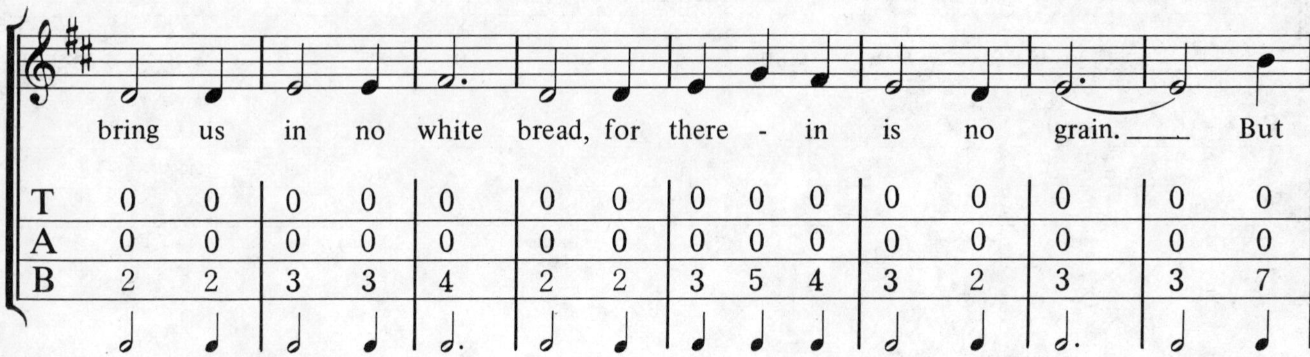


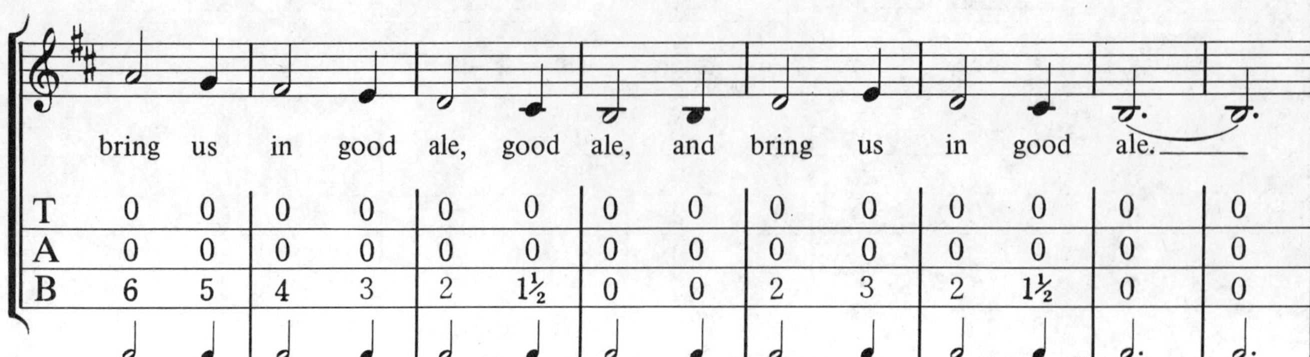

Bring us in no eggs,
for there are many shells.
But bring us in good ale and
bring us nothing else.

**Chorus:**
But bring us in good ale, good ale
And bring us in good ale.
For our blessed lady's sake,
Bring us in good ale.

Bring us in no mutton,
for that is often lean,
Nor bring us in no trypes,
for they be seldom clean.

**Chorus:**

Bring us in no capon's flesh,
for that is often dear,
Nor bring us in no duck's flesh
that slobber in the mire.

**Chorus:**

Bring us in no butter,
for that is full of hairs,
Nor bring us in no pig's flesh,
for that will make us boars.

**Chorus:**

## FAREWELL TO GALAPAGOS

Due to a shortage of music composed in the Phrygian mode, I've decided to write one myself.

Tune to DD-A-D and capo the 5th fret. You can play the melody on the bass string if you wish.

By Neal Hellman

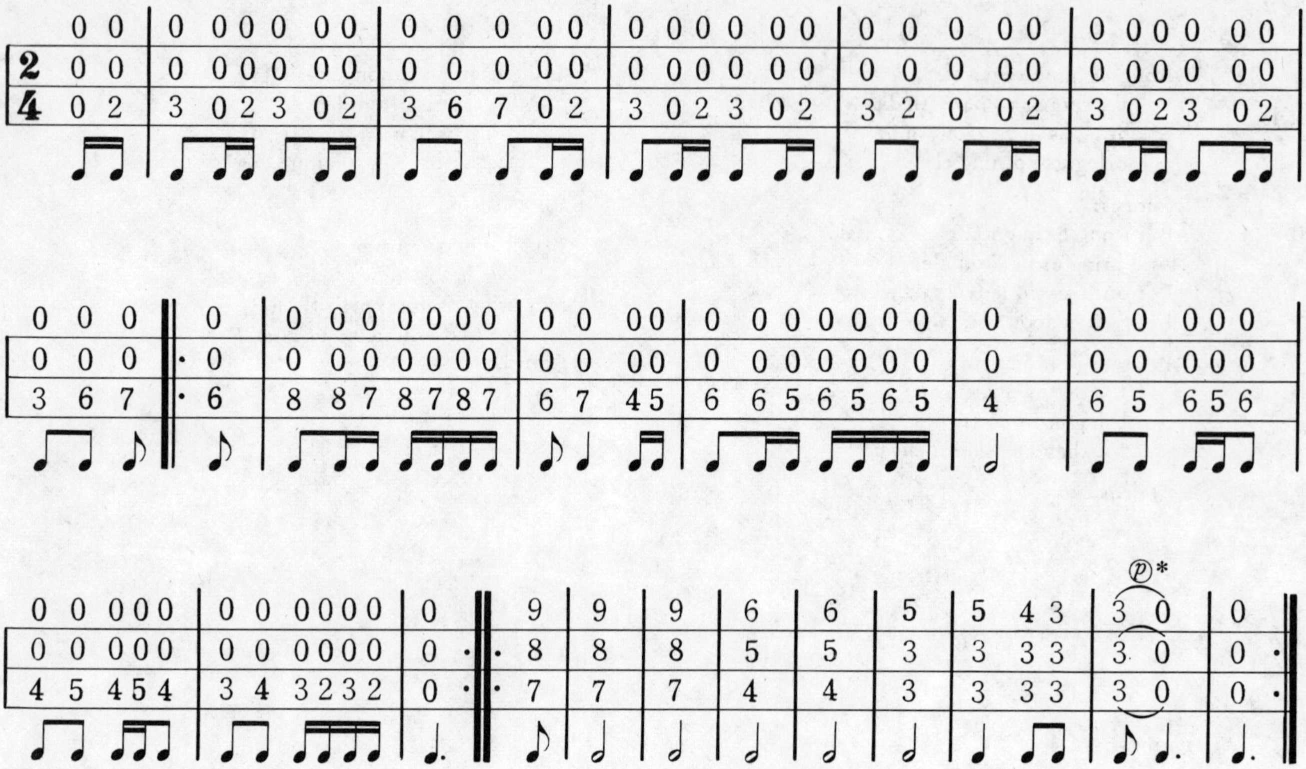

```
  0 0 | 0 000 0 00 | 0 0 0 00 | 0 000 0 00 | 0 0 0 00 | 0 000 0 00 |
2 0 0 | 0 000 0 00 | 0 0 0 00 | 0 000 0 00 | 0 0 0 00 | 0 000 0 00 |
4 0 2 | 3 023 0 2  | 3 6 7 0 2| 3 023 0 2  | 3 2 0 0 2| 3 023 0 2  |

0 0 0 ||  0 | 0 0000000 | 0 0 00 | 0 000000 0 | 0 | 0 0 000 |
0 0 0 ||: 0 | 0 0000000 | 0 0 00 | 0 000000 0 | 0 | 0 0 000 |
3 6 7 ||: 6 | 8 8787 87 | 6 7 45 | 6 656565 5 | 4 | 6 5 656 |

0 0 000 | 0 0 0000 | 0  ||  9 | 9 | 9 | 6 | 6 | 5 | 5 43 | 3 0 | 0  ||
0 0 000 | 0 0 0000 | 0 :||: 8 | 8 | 8 | 5 | 5 | 3 | 3 33 | 3 0 | 0 :||
4 5 454 | 3 4 3232 | 0 :||: 7 | 7 | 7 | 4 | 4 | 3 | 3 33 | 3 0 | 0 :||
```



*Pull-off.

## THE WOODS SO WILD

Now, in the DD-A-D tuning we place our capo to the left of the 6th fret and we arrive in the C Lydian Mode. Here we have the same scale as the Ionian except the 4th note of the scale is *sharp*. We will now be in a C tuning. With the capo our scale starts on the open note or strum. If you're in a *standard* Lydian tuning (EE-A-D) or DD-G-C) your scale would start on the 6th fret. "Allen's Interlude" by Richard Fariña is in this mode.

This piece is taken from the 16th century "Fitzwilliam Virginal Book." Before starting, you should skip ahead and read the instructions for the fingerpicking chapter. You can, of course, just strum the tune with or without the chords, but I like it better using a combination of pinches and strums. Wherever you see all three lines with numbers: **2/0/0**, it means you *strum* across all the strings while fretting the string indicated.

Traditional
Arranged by Neal and Sally Hellman

Capo 6th fret

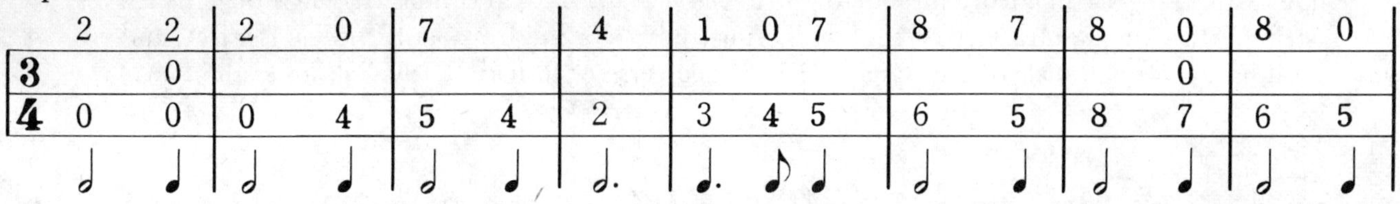

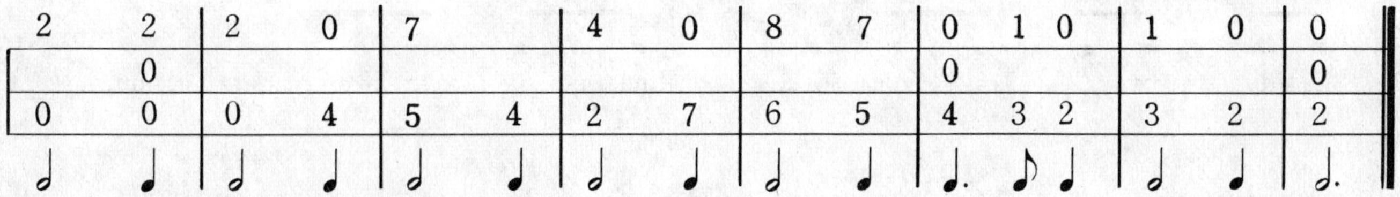

```
    2   2 | 2   0 | 7     | 4     | 1   0 7 | 8   7 | 8   0 | 8   0 |
3       0 |       |       |       |         |       |     0 |       |
4   0   0 | 0   4 | 5   4 | 2     | 3   4 5 | 6   5 | 8   7 | 6   5 |
    ♩   ♩ | ♩   ♩ | ♩   ♩ | ♩.    | ♩.  ♪ ♩ | ♩   ♩ | ♩   ♩ | ♩   ♩ |
   (half, quarter; dotted half = ♩. in measure 4)

    2   2 | 2   0 | 7     | 4   0 | 8   7 | 0   1 0 | 1   0 | 0 ||
        0 |       |       |       |       | 0       |       | 0 ||
    0   0 | 0   4 | 5   4 | 2   7 | 6   5 | 4   3 2 | 3   2 | 2 ||
```

Rhythm, line 1: half, quarter | half, quarter | half, quarter | dotted half | dotted quarter, eighth, quarter | half, quarter | half, quarter | half, quarter

Rhythm, line 2: half, quarter | half, quarter | half, quarter | half, quarter | half, quarter | dotted quarter, eighth, quarter | half, quarter | dotted half

# The Versatile Lydian Mode

Due to its sharped fourth, the Lydian Mode has not been used very often in traditional and contemporary music. On the dulcimer it has a lot more to offer than what first meets the ear. So let's tune to this mode and then explore its possibilities.

Tune your bass string to the desired tone. For our example let us use C. Press down the bass string just to the left of the 4th fret and tune the middle string to it. Now press the bass string just to the left of the 8th fret and tune the melody strings to it. You are now tuned for a Lydian Mode of C (DD-G-C). The scale starts on the 6th fret of the melody strings. Starting at the 6th fret the scale would be: C, D, E, F♯, G, A, B, C. Experiment around with this scale for a while. "The Woods So Wild," which is a piece written out in the Lydian Mode and appeared at the end of the capo section just preceding, might be interesting to try now without the capo.
Richard Fariña wrote two tunes in the Lydian Mode: "Miles" and "Allen's Interlude." But he used the "extra" fret and composed them in the Mixolydian and Ionian tunings respectively. As you now know, you can also capo into the Lydian Mode from DD-A-D tuning by capoing on the 6th fret.

One can also play in a Dorian Mode of G (in the present Lydian tuning DD-G-C) on the bass string. Start on the 4th fret of the bass string and go up the fretboard to the 11th fret, and you have a Dorian scale of G ("Gm"). Here is one verse of "Shady Grove" as an example.

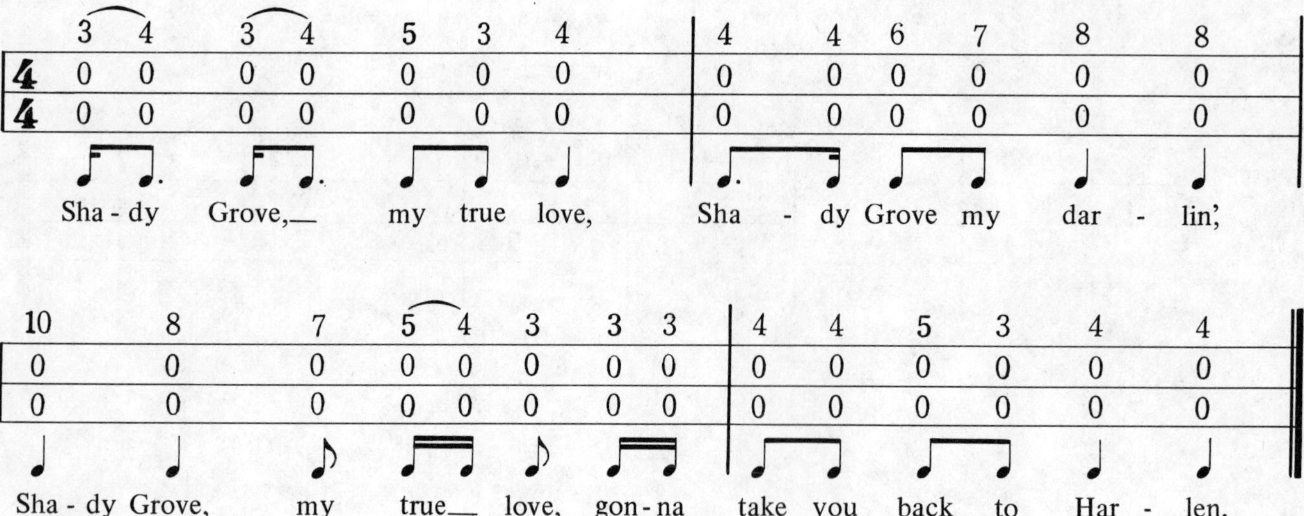


Try any Dorian tune you know this way, and I am sure you'll find it fun to play the melody on the bass string. Be sure, though, to "angle" your pick in such a way that you don't get too much drone from the first strings.

This Lydian tuning is useful also for the many chords it contains. One can use this Mode for "backing-up" fast tunes or just strumming to accompany your singing. By utilizing the following chords one can play rhythm or "back-up" in almost any key. These chords are for C Lydian tuning (DD-G-C).

| Chord | Top | Middle | Bottom |
|---|---|---|---|
| G | 4 4 6½ | 2 4 0 | 0 5 0 |
| G Modal | 4 | 0 | 0 |
| G7 | 4 | 6 | 5 |
| Gm | 6 6 0 | 7 4 6 | 0 3 4 |
| G Maj7 | 4 5 | 6 3 | 5 3 |
| C | 0 2 0 7 | 0 3 5 5 | 3 3 6 6 |
| C Modal | 0 | 0 | 1 |
| C9 | 4 2 | 5 3 | 0 0 |
| D | 1 | 1 | 2 |
| D Modal | 1 5 5 | 1 4 4 | 0 4 0 |
| Dm | 5 3 | 6 4 | 0 0 |
| Dm7 | 7 | 6 | 0 |
| D9 | 6 | 5 | 0 |
| E Modal | 2 | 2 | 1 |
| Em | 2 | 2 | 3 |
| Em7 | 4 | 5 | 0 |
| E9 | 2 | 2 | 2 |
| F | 3 5 | 3 6 | 4 6 |
| F6 | 3 | 3 | 0 |
| F9 | 5 | 3 | 3 |
| A | 5 | 5 | 6½ |
| A Modal | 5 | 5 | 4 |
| Am | 5 | 5 | 6 |
| Am7 | 5 | 7 | 6 |
| Asus | 2 5 | 1 5 | 0 0 |
| B♭ | 6 | 6 | 0 |
| Bm | 1 6½ | 2 6½ | 2 7 |
| B♭m | 6 | 6 | 7 |

Start with just the basic chords, and then work on incorporating ones you don't use too often like Em7th or Asus4. An easy way to explore these chords is to start with D Major: 1/1/2 and work your way up to 2/2/3, 3/3/4, and so on. The next tune ("Fiddler A' Dram") is an example of using the Lydian mode as a back-up to either a lead instrument or your voice.

## FIDDLER A' DRAM

Tune to the Lydian Mode of C (DD-G-C). The chords one makes in this tuning, however, will be for the key of G. The melody is written out on the *middle* string; it is only there to show you how the tune goes. So just pluck the middle string by itself to get the melody. The chords are as follows:

| | G | F | C | D | A |
|---|---|---|---|---|---|
| | 4 | 3 | 0 | 1 | 5 |
| = | 4 | 3 | 0 | 1 | 5 |
| | 0 | 0 | 1 | 0 | 6½* |

Traditional
In the style of Rick Scott

*If you don't have a 6½ fret, use A Modal: 5/5/4.

Sugar in the gourd, gourd in the ground.
If you want to get the sugar
you've got to kick the gourd around. *(2x)*

Hound dog gone, Jenny come along,
Pretty little girl with the red dress on.
She took it off, I took it on,
Twenty long years since she's been gone.

**Chorus:**
Dram, dram, the fiddler a dram,
Come on and give the fiddler a dram. *(2x)*

**Bridge:**
Get drunk all night don't give a damn,
Get drunk all night and don't give a damn,
Get drunk all night and don't give a damn,
Come on and give the fiddler a dram.

Jawbone walk, Jawbone talk,
Jawbone eat with a knife and fork. *(2x)*

Left my jawbone on a fence,
Haven't seen a damn thing since.
Dance all night with a bottle in my hand,
Come on and give the fiddler a dram.

**Chorus:**

**Bridge:**

# Playing in a Major Key While in Dorian Tuning

## CARELESS LOVE

Tune your dulcimer to any standard Dorian Mode. For this example we will use the Dorian tuning for E ("Em"), AA-B-E. By making certain chord patterns one can play in a major key. Although somewhat handy, it is limiting, due to the fact that we can only play rhythm and not a major scale. The melody is written below the chords for E Ionian (E Major) tuning (BB-B-E) so you can tell how the tune goes, and can have a friend play it in E Ionian while you strum the chords (in E Dorian tuning, sounding as E Ionian). The chords:

| | | | | | |
|---|---|---|---|---|---|
| | 2 | | 3 | | 4 |
| E = | 3 | A = | 3 | B7 = | 0 |
| | 1 | | 2 | | 5 |

Traditional
Arranged by Neal and Sally Hellman

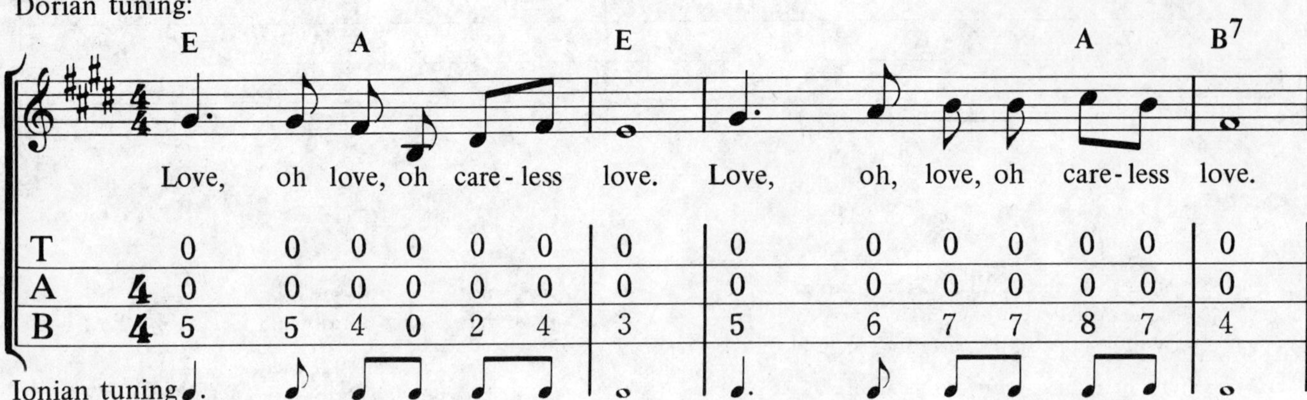


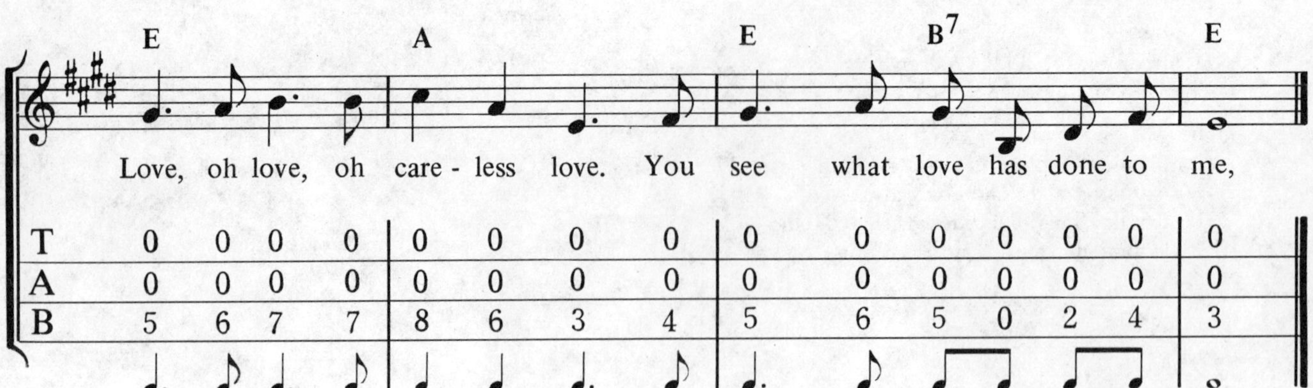




Other Major chords in the Dorian Mode:

| | | | | | | | | | |
|---|---|---|---|---|---|---|---|---|---|
| | 4 | 7 | 10 | | 8 | | 5 | | 6 |
| E = | 5 or | 5 or | 11 | B7 = | 9 | A = | 6 | D = | 6 |
| | 4 | 8 | 8 | | 8 | | 4 | | 5 |

# III. Fingerpicking on the Dulcimer

In August of 1975 I attended the first "kindred gathering" (dulcimer festival) in the state of Washington. Many styles and approaches to the dulcimer were displayed there. However, not one person was fingerpicking the dulcimer. Not many people do; why, I don't know. But to fingerpick the dulcimer is to create an entirely different mood, flavor and tone-coloring. Fingerpicking changes the disposition of the instrument and the player. Listen to some of Roger Nicholson's and Kevin Roth's records (listed in the back) and hear the delicacy one can create by fingerpicking.

The fingerpicking tab here will be similar to the strumming songs you've seen already. The strings will be represented by staff lines with the top line representing the bass string. All four-string dulcimers will be represented by three lines, where the bottom line shows the first two strings.

All the picking can be done with the thumb and index fingers of your right hand. One might want to add the middle finger, once you get familiar with the tunes. Most of the fretting can be done with the thumb, index and middle fingers. You will sometimes need all of your fingers for fretting once you get into more involved work.

Some new symbols:

Ⓢ 2 – 1 means to *slide* your fretting finger from the 2nd fret to the first without lifting it off the fretboard.

3 / 5 means to play the 3rd fret of the bass string and the 5th fret of the first string at the same time, thus creating a *"pinch."*

3 / 4 / 5 Here, you could either pluck all three strings together, or just use a strum.

Ⓗ 0 1 means to *"hammer-on"* the first fret. One would hit the fret directly after plucking the string.

Ⓟ 1 0 means to *"pull-off."* Pluck the string while your finger is on the 1st fret. Right after you pluck it, pull your finger off so the open string will sound.

## SHADY GROVE

Here's a good example of fingerpicking in the Aeolian Mode while tuned to the standard Mixolydian. So tune your dulcimer to D Mixolydian (DD-A-D) and, by making the following positions you'll be playing in an Aeolian Mode of E (Em).

Traditional
Arranged by Neal and Sally Hellman

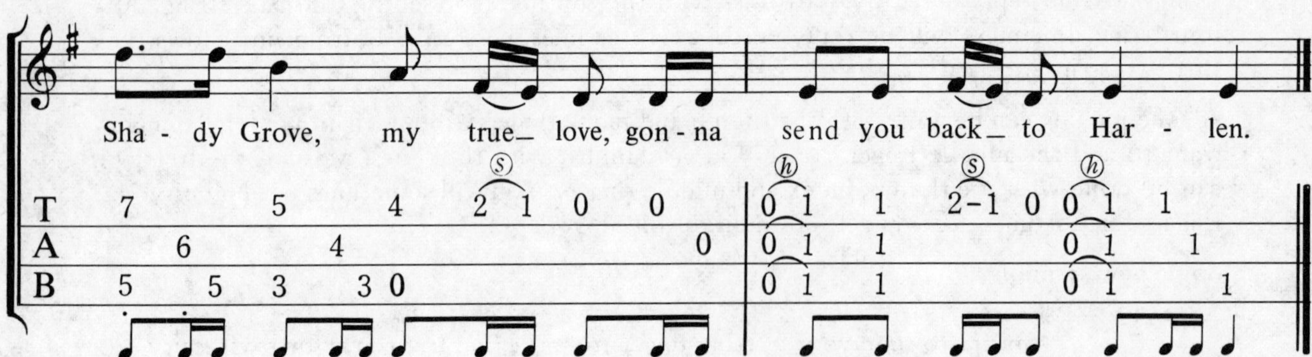


Yonder stands my Shady Grove,
Standing by the door.
Shoes and stockings in her hand,
Little bare feet on the floor.

Wish I had a big old horse,
Corn to feed him on,
Pretty little Miss to stay at home
And feed him when I'm gone.

Peaches in the summertime,
Apples in the fall,
If I can't have the one I love
I won't have no one at all.

Some come here to fiddle and dance,
Some come here to marry,
Some come here to fiddle and dance,
I come here to marry.

Wish I had a banjo string
Made of golden twine,
And every tune I'd pick on it
Is "I wish that girl were mine."

# THE PRICKLE HOLLY BUSH

Written for the standard D Mixolydian: DD-A-D. Remember to reverse the middle and bass strings of the tab to play in the New Mixolydian. A Hampshire folk song also known as "Hangman" or "The Maid Freed from the Gallows Tree." The voice is in the key of D.

Traditional
Arranged by Neal and Sally Hellman

2. Hangman stay your rope,
Will you stay it for some while?
For I think I see my father coming,
Riding over yonder mile.

3. Father, did you bring me gold
Or silver to set me free,
For to save my body from the cold clay ground,
My neck from the gallows tree?

4. I've not brought you gold
Or silver to set you free,
For I have come to see you hanging
High on the gallows tree.

**Chorus:**
Oh the prickle-holly bush
It pricks my poor heart sore,
And if I ever get out of the prickle-holly bush
I'll never get in it anymore.



5, 6 &7. *Same as verses 2, 3 & 4, except use "brother" wherever you see "father."*

**Chorus:**

8&9 *Use "lover."*

10. Yes, I've brought you gold
And silver to set you free,
To save thy body from the cold, clay ground
And thy neck from the gallows tree.

**Chorus:**

## SKYE BOAT SONG

Tune to any standard Mixolydian tuning (DD-A-D, CC-G-C, etc.) to play this Scottish air. A combination of "pinches" and solo notes seems to go well with the song.

Traditional
Arranged by Neal and Sally Hellman

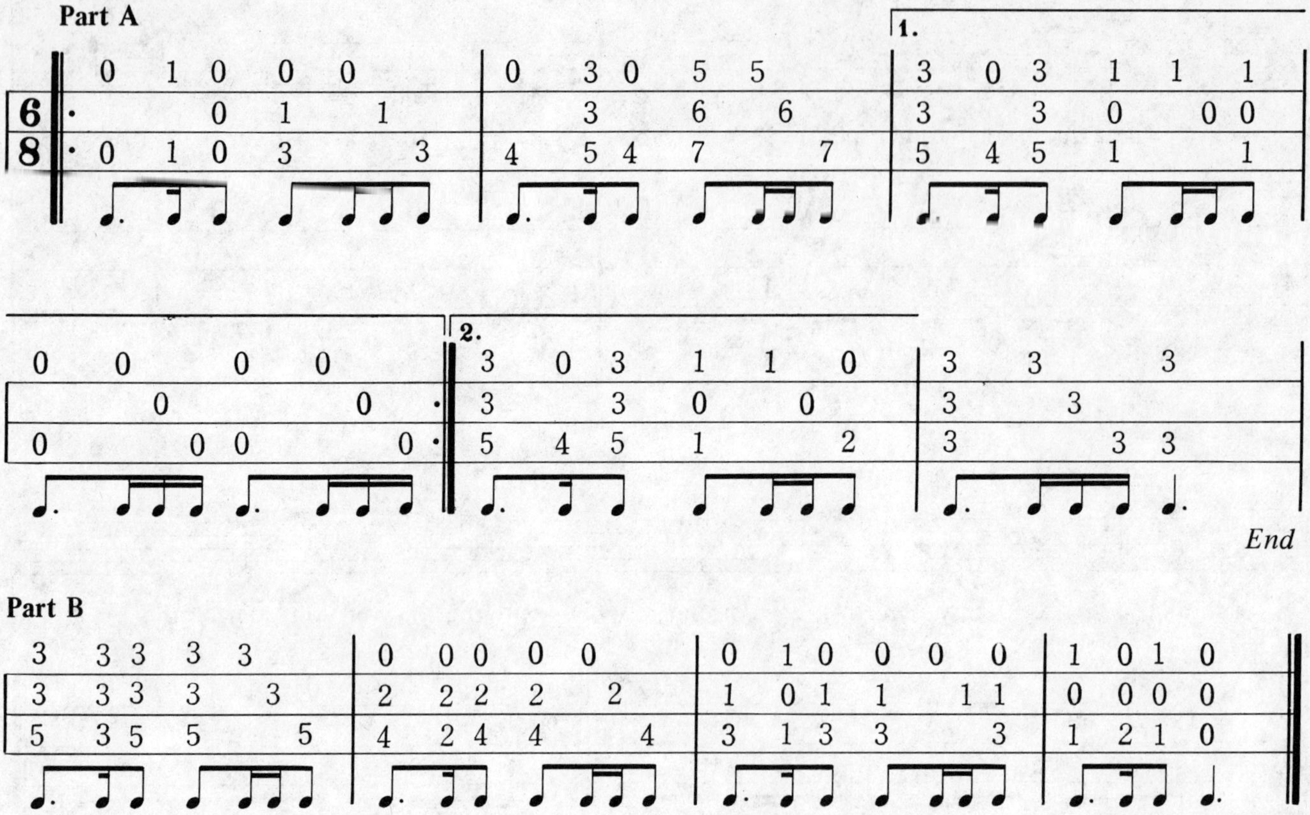

**Part A**

```
                                                 1.
   0  1 0   0  0     |  0   3 0  5  5     |  3  0 3   1  1  1  |
6            0  1  1 |      3    6    6   |  3    3   0    0 0 |
8  0  1 0   3      3 |  4   5 4  7     7  |  5  4 5   1      1 |

                                2.
 0   0     0   0     ||  3   0 3   1  1   0  |  3   3     3
       0          0 :||  3     3   0     0   |  3     3
 0       0 0      0 :||  5   4 5   1       2 |  3         3 3
                                                              End
```

**Part B**

```
 3   3 3  3  3      |  0  0 0  0  0     |  0  1 0  0  0  0  |  1  0 1  0  ||
 3   3 3  3    3    |  2  2 2  2    2   |  1  0 1  1    1 1 |  0  0 0  0  ||
 5   3 5  5      5  |  4  2 4  4      4 |  3  1 3  3      3 |  1  2 1  0  ||
```

*Repeat Part A once through, using the 2nd ending.*



## WEDDING DRESS SONG

Written out in the standard D Aeolian Mode (Dm), tuned CC-A-D. Don't get flustered by all the numbers and notes. Once you know the melody and follow the tab you shouldn't have any problem. After you learn this version try arranging one by yourself.

I have heard this tune from a number of records and people, but I think they all go back to the arrangement of Aunt Molly Jackson.

**WEDDING DRESS SONG**

Traditional
Arranged by Neal and Sally Hellman

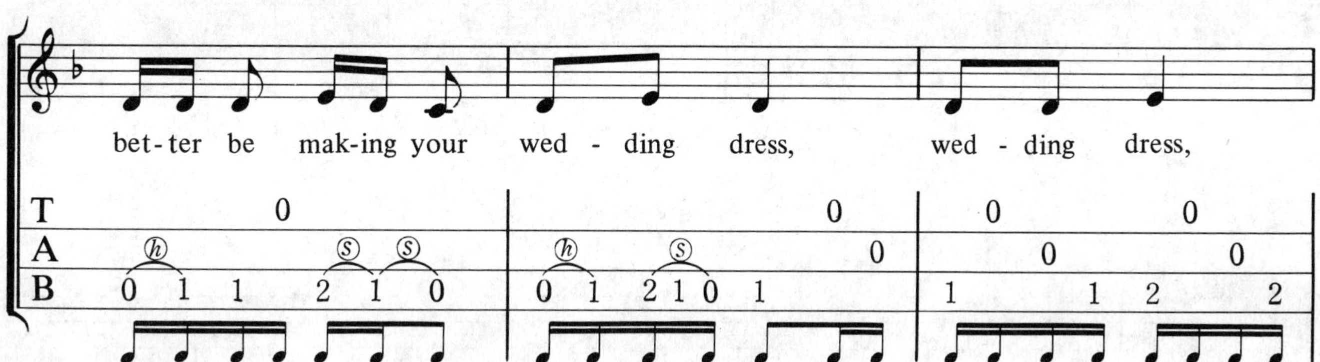


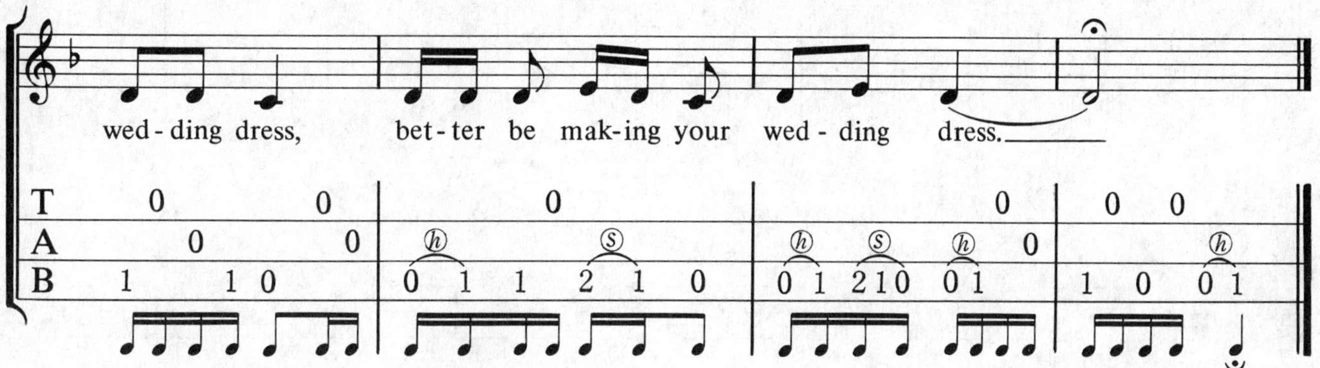


Well, it's already made, trimmed in brown,
Stitched around with a golden crown,
Golden crown, golden crown,
Stitched around with a golden crown.

Well, it's already made, trimmed in green,
Prettiest thing you've ever seen,
Ever seen, ever seen,
Prettiest thing you've ever seen.

Well, its already made, trimmed in white,
Gonna be married on Saturday night,
Saturday night, Saturday night,
Gonna be married on Saturday night.



Well, she wouldn't say yes, wouldn't say no,
All she'd do is just sit and sew,
Sit and sew, sit and sew,
All she'd do is just sit and sew.

Hey, my little dony gal,
Don't you guess,
Better be makin' your wedding dress,
Wedding dress, wedding dress,
Better be makin' your wedding dress.

## SERVING GIRL'S HOLIDAY

Written out for the New Mixolydian tuning: AA-A-E ("A Major"). You know what to do by now to change it to standard Mixolydian tuning. The voice part is in A Major.

Play the introduction between each verse and again at the end of the song.

Traditional
Arranged by Neal and Sally Hellman

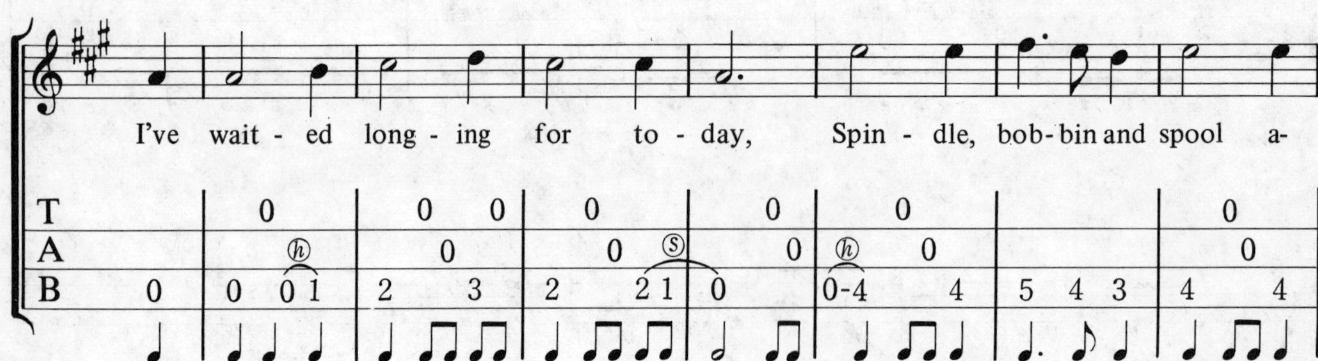


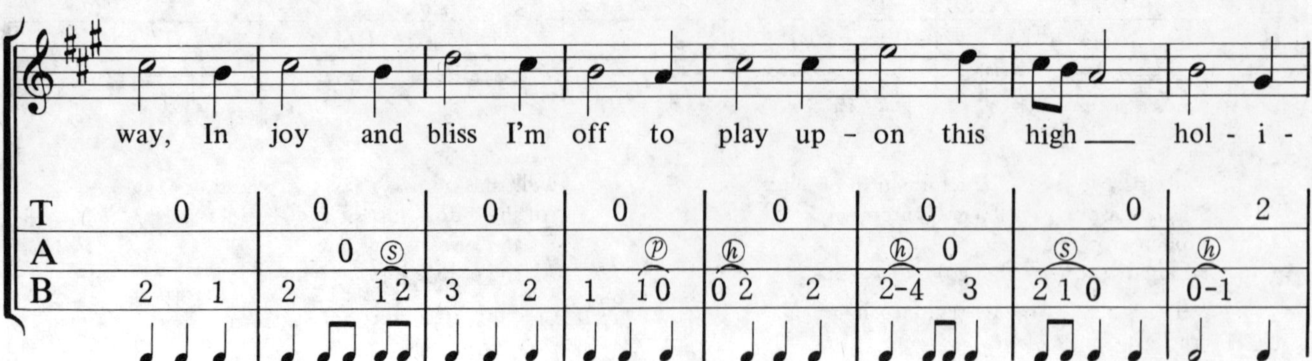

The dirt upon the floor's unswept,
The fireplace isn't clean and kept,
I haven't cut the rushes yet,
Upon this high holiday.

**Chorus:**
And spindle, bobbin and spool away,
But joy that it's a holiday.

In pails the milk has got to go,
I ought to spread this bowl of dough,
It clogs my nails and fingers so,
As I knead this high holiday.

**Chorus:**

The cooking herbs I must fetch in,
And fix my kerchief under my chin.
Darling Jack, lend me a pin
To fix me well this holiday.

**Chorus:**

I've waited longing for today,
Spindle, bobbin and spool away,
In joy and bliss I'm off to play
Upon this high holiday.

**Chorus:**

Bonnie Carol

## THE RIGHTS OF MAN
(Hornpipe)

---

Tune to the standard Mixolydian (DD-A-D for this example). By utilizing the following chords we will be picking this tune in the Aeolian Mode of E (Em). When playing with a fiddle or banjo who is going pretty fast just play the chords (Em, G, D). I find it very pretty just to slowly fingerpick some jigs and hornpipes. This one is a very powerful tune, as you can see:

Traditional
In the style of
Teddy McKnight and Ruthie Beanenfeld

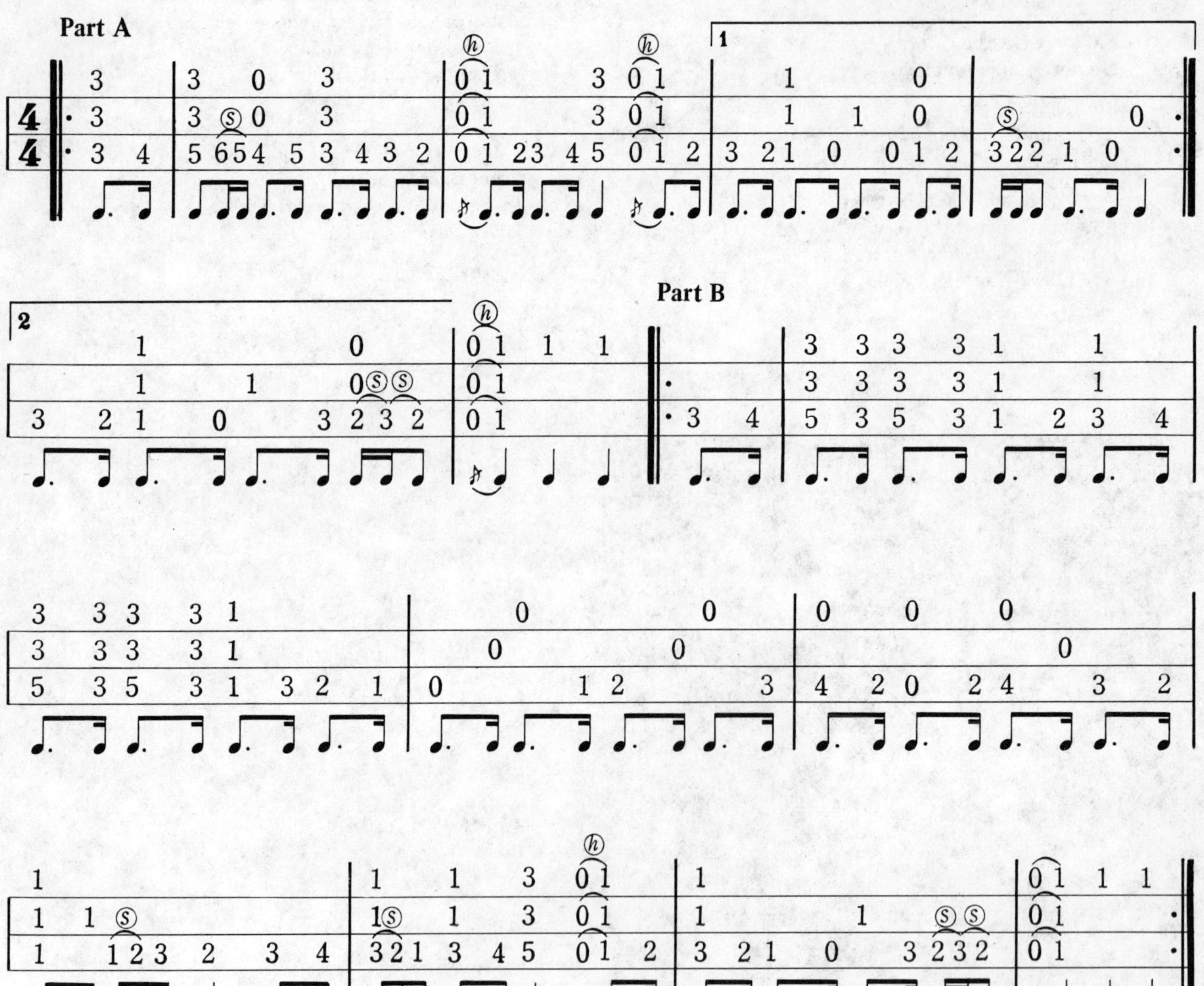

## LOCH LAVAN CASTLE

Use any standard Mixolydian tuning, say DD-A-D, our usual example; with the positions, notes, and chords you make you'll be playing in an Aeolian Mode of E (if you're tuned to DD-A-D). As you see, the "extra" fret is needed. If you're lacking one you can fake it by leaving that string open, but it will not sound as good.

The only record I've heard this on is "The Fuzzy Mountain String Band," though that version is a little different.

*Reminder:* When you see a single note on a line, you just pick that string. When there are two strings with numbers (1/3) you pluck those two strings simultaneously. When all three strings are numbered, you can either pluck all three, or just strum.

Traditional
In the style of Teddy McKnight

**Part A**

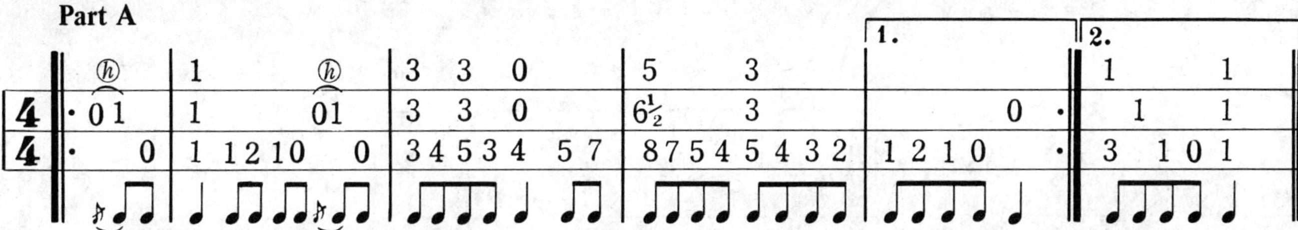

**Part B**

| | | | | |
|---|---|---|---|---|
| | 5 3 | 5 0 | 5 3 | |
| | 6½ 3 | 6½ 0 | 6½ 3 | |
| 5 7 | 8 7 5 4 3 4 5 7 | 8 7 543 4 5 7 | 8 7 5 4 5 4 3 2 | 1 2 1 1 |

*Repeat part A, using 2nd ending.*

## LANNAGAN'S BALL JIG

Tuned to standard D Mixolydian (DD-A-D). You'll once again be playing in an Aeolian Mode of E (Em). I would suggest for the barre chords you try your middle three fingers. For the "strum" try: forward–back–forward or back–forward–back. If you don't have the 6½ fret use the 6th fret and you'll do OK.

Traditional
In the style of Teddy McKnight

**Part A**

```
| 1     1   | 3    3     | 0     0  | 0  0002  || 5    4  | 1      1 |
| 1      1  |   3  3     | 0     0  |          || 6    4  | 1       1|
| 1013   4  | 5  456½7   | 0102  3  | 475420   || 875654  | 3101   1 |
```

**Part B**

```
| 1   1        | 0 00     | 1   1     | 2   2      || 5    4  | 1      1 |
| 11  1(S)(S)  | 0        | 11  1     | 1  1101    || 6    4  | 1     1  |
| 1  2321      | 243210   | 1  2321   | 20         || 875654  | 3101     |
```

Kevin Roth

## SIR SHYALOTT

Standard Mixolydian tuning. This is mainly just a combination of pinches and single-note picking. The main pattern is: pinch (melody and bass)–pick (middle)–pick (melody string.)

By Neal Hellman

**Part A**

**Part B**

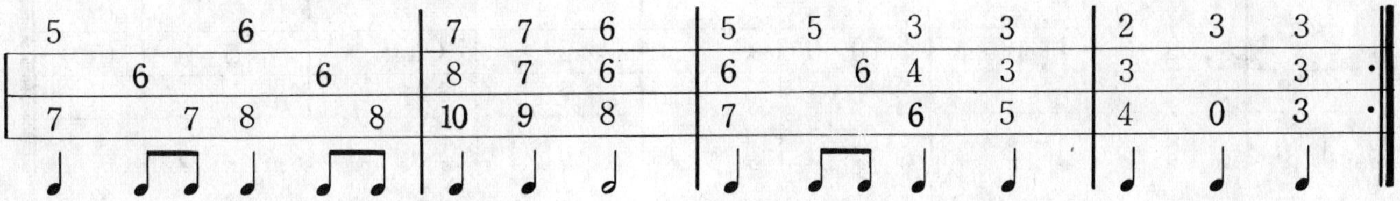

## THE SWALLOWTAIL JIG
(Flat-picked version)

Best done in the New Aeolian tuning (GG-A-E [Am] or AA-B-F♯[Bm] ), although the tune is in Dorian. Reverse the middle and bass strings if you want to play in the standard Aeolian tuning. Use a firm but not hard flatpick. Pick all the notes, and strum where you see chords.

This sounds great with a guitar in the background to hold down the rhythm. You're wondering why a jig is written out in waltz time. This version is meant to give the dulcimer the "lead." In 6/8 time you'd have to pick so fast that you'd lose the lilt of the tune.

This is similar to the playing of Margaret MacArthur on *On the Mountains High,* (Living Folk Records, F-LFR-100).

Traditional
In the style of Margaret MacArthur

**Part A**

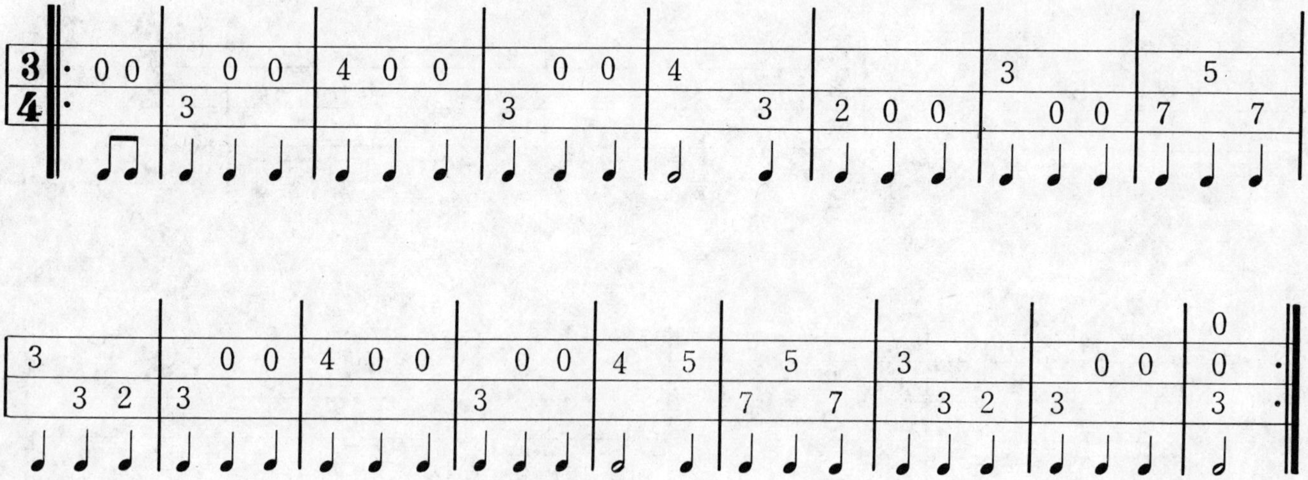

**Part B**

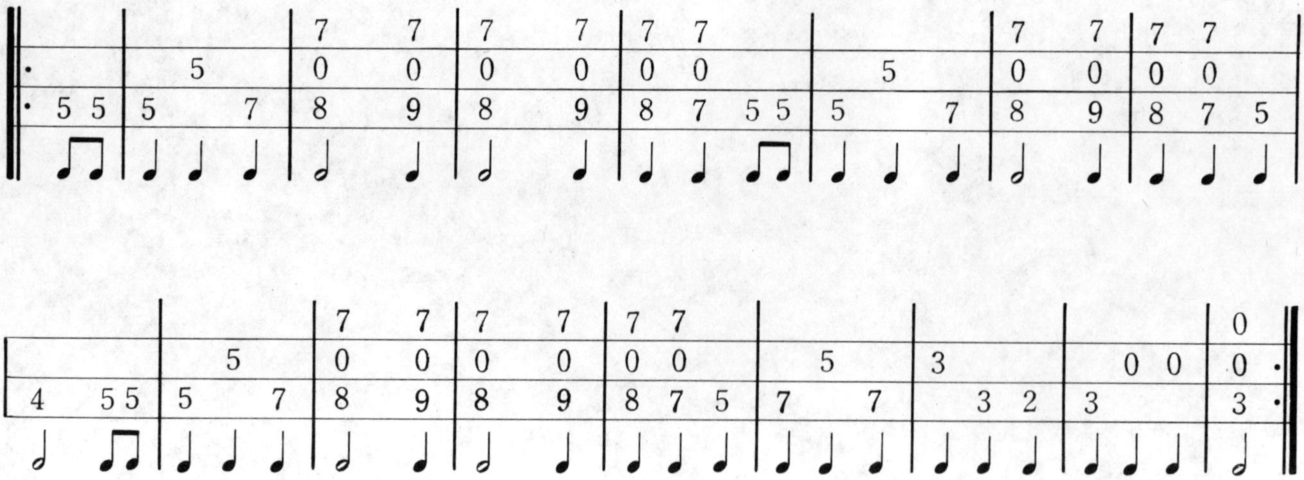

# JENNY LIND POLKA

Tune dulcimer to any "New" Ionian Mode, (DD-G-D). Use a flatpick or, if you wish, your fingers. You may strum completely across all the strings where it sounds good, such as in a position like 0/4/5.

This is from the playing of Margaret MacArthur on the album *Old Songs* (Philo Records 1001).

Traditional
Arranged by Margaret MacArthur

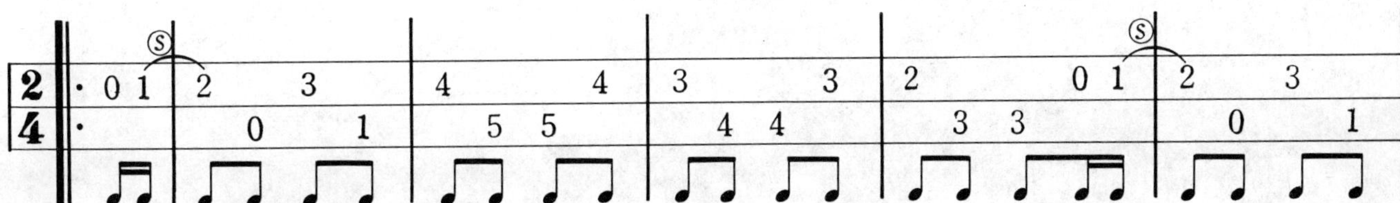

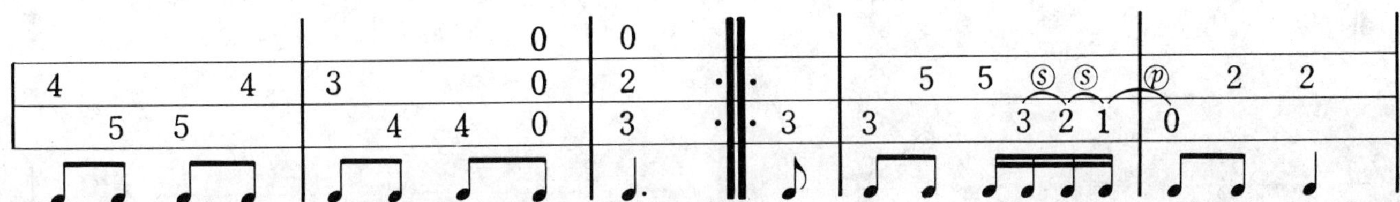

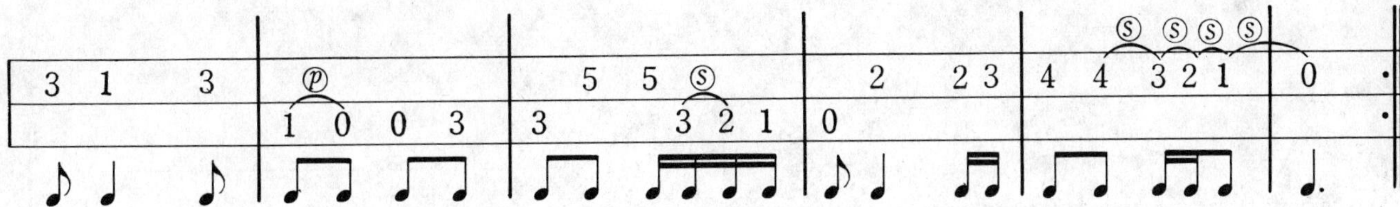

## POKER FACE SMILE

Two sleight-of-hands maintain the balance in this song. First, each successive phrase adds one new element to the syncopation, building toward a perfect rhythmic round. Secondly, broken-chord flatpicking (arpeggios) adds movement to the harmony; each note of the chord is individually played in sequence from bass to treble. The whole song could be played with a simple 1-3-2-1 repeated pattern where the first (melody string) is picked away from you. However, the song could also be strummed throughout. By themselves, both flatpicking and strumming limit this song by making it too regular, even boring. Used together, interest is added and the simple lilt of the song preserved.

Play the chorus an octave higher. Tuning: DD–A–D.

Words and music
by Robert Force

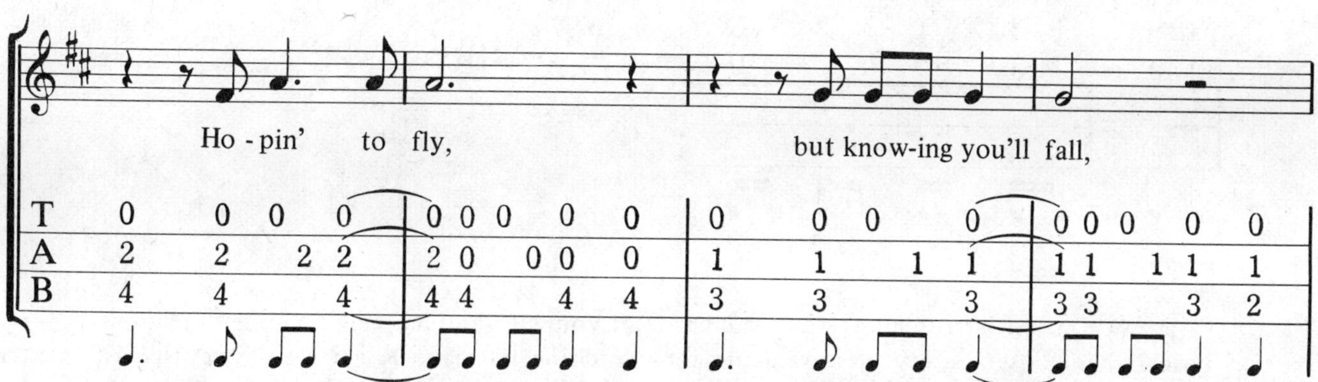


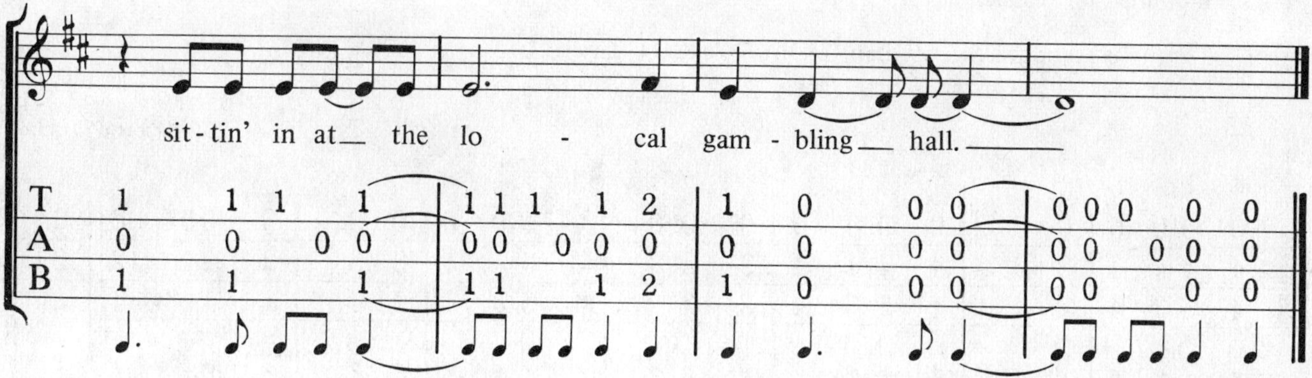


Take a lot of notes
to pay for that game,
Take a lot of music
to make me sane.
Take a lot of miles
of sunshine and rain
'til I'm back on the
winning side again.

After you've played
life's one last card,
The way down that road
won't seem quite so hard.
When you've turned your back on
bright lights and bars,
And opened yourself
to what you are.

**Chorus:**
Child of morning
with tomorrow's eyes,
Child of living
nobody's lies,
Child of laughter
with nothin' to hide,
A child of
living the beauty inside.

And smoke-filled rooms
hold nothing for you,
And no words reach you
but those that ring true.
And you cry for the people
with nothin' to do,
But hope for an ace
to pull them on thru.

They're looking for something
so high and so wild,
That all they can see
is cunning and guile.
They've no time to listen
to the voice of the child,
They've hidden behind their
poker face smile.

**Chorus:**

## CORNWALL

The fingerpicking tab for *Cornwall* will be a little different from the previous tunes. In songs like "The Wedding Dress Song" every movement was written out. In this composition we will give the chord position in tab and the suggested fingerpicking style separately. Since it is the same for most of the tune we found it less complicated than writing out every movement.

The fingerpicking style (1 is the melody string, 2 the middle and 3 the bass):

**Picking pattern:**

```
               1  3  2  1  3  2  1  3
 0 0              0        0        0
|4 4|   |         4        4         |
|4 5| = | 4          4        5      |
```

"Cornwall" is an instrumental study—an etude, if you will—emphasizing a strong but simple lyrical theme. As a study, it is valuable for exercising left-hand finger technique; that is, keeping the fingers on the fretboard while slowly, delicately voicing the melody without overdroning—the bane of so much dulcimer music. Played wistfully, it transports well. Remember to breathe.

Tuning is standard Mixolydian (DD-A-D or CC-G-C, etc.).

By Albert d'Ossché.

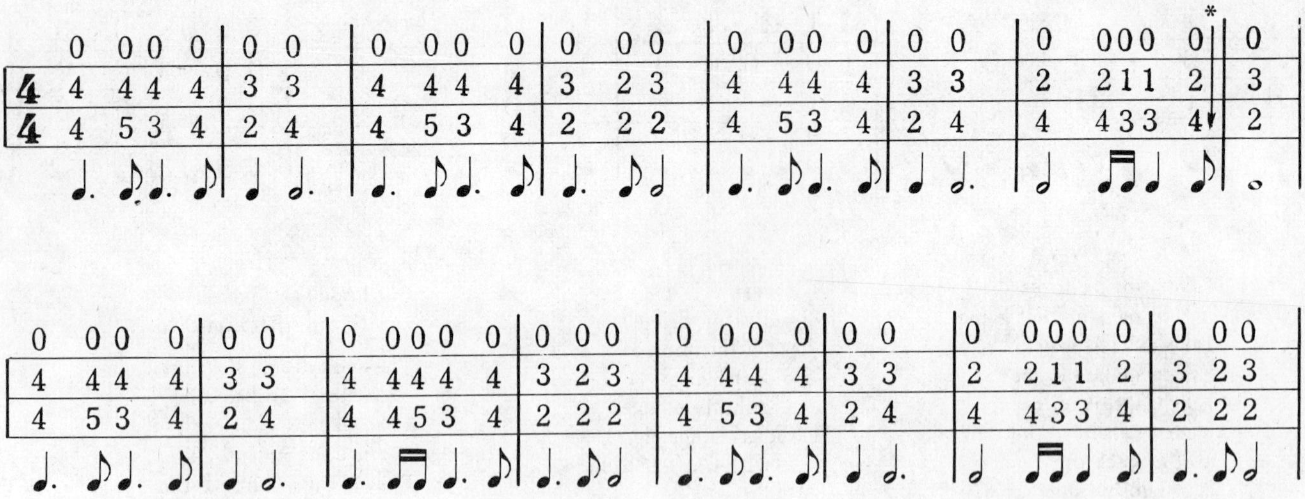

```
                                                                     *
    0  00 0 | 0 0 | 0  00  0 | 0  00 | 0  00  0 | 0 0 | 0  000  0 | 0
4   4  44 4 | 3 3 | 4  44  4 | 3  23 | 4  44  4 | 3 3 | 2  211  2 | 3
4   4  53 4 | 2 4 | 4  53  4 | 2  22 | 4  53  4 | 2 4 | 4  433  4↓| 2
```

```
0  00  0 | 0 0 | 0 000 0 | 0 00 | 0 00 0 | 0 0 | 0  000 0 | 0 00
4  44  4 | 3 3 | 4 444 4 | 3 23 | 4 44 4 | 3 3 | 2  211 2 | 3 23
4  53  4 | 2 4 | 4 453 4 | 2 22 | 4 53 4 | 2 4 | 4  433 4 | 2 22
```



*Brush down on all strings with index finger.

| 0 0 0 0 | 0 0** | 0 00 000 | 0 | 0 00 0 | 0 0 | 0 0 0 000 | 0 |
|---|---|---|---|---|---|---|---|
| 5 6 7 6 | 5 6 | 6 76 656 | 7 | 5 67 6 | 5 6 | 6 7 8 756 | 7 |
| 7 8 9 8 | 7 5 | 8 98 545 | 7 | 7 89 8 | 7 5 | 8 9 10 978 | 7 |

| 0 00 0 | 0 0 | 0 00 0 | 0 00 | 0 00 0 | 0 0 | 0 0 0 | 000 |
|---|---|---|---|---|---|---|---|
| 4 44 4 | 3 3 | 4 44 4 | 3 23 | 4 44 4 | 3 3 | 2 1 2 | 5 6 7 |
| 4 53 4 | 2 4 | 4 53 4 | 2 22 | 4 53 4 | 2 4 | 4 3 4 | 7 7 7 |

L to R: Albert d'Ossché, Robert Force, Neal Hellman

**Brush down on 1st two strings and pluck bass string.

## EVERYTHING'S FINE RIGHT NOW

As well as being a beautiful song this also presents us with another good example of playing in one mode and key while tuned to another. For this song we tune to the standard Lydian Mode of C, which is DD-G-C. However, by using certain chords and positions one can play in the key of G Major while in standard Lydian tuning.

The following style will fit this tune:

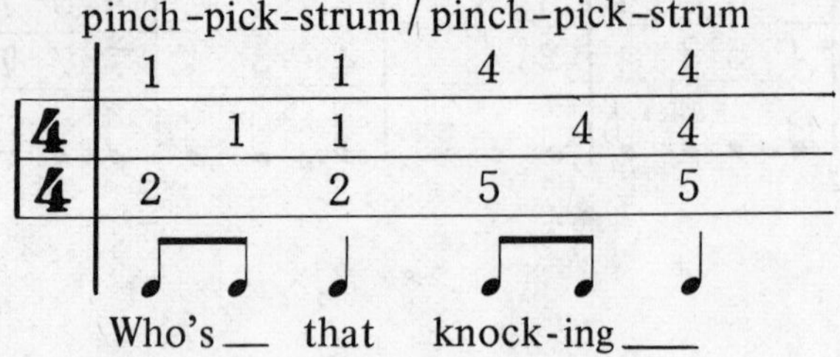


You can do the rest of the song in the same style except for two places:

1. The fourth measure, which is: pinch-pick-strum-strum.
2. The twelfth measure ("really love the best") which is: pinch-pick-pinch-pick-strum.

Words and music by Mike Heron
Arranged by Rick Scott

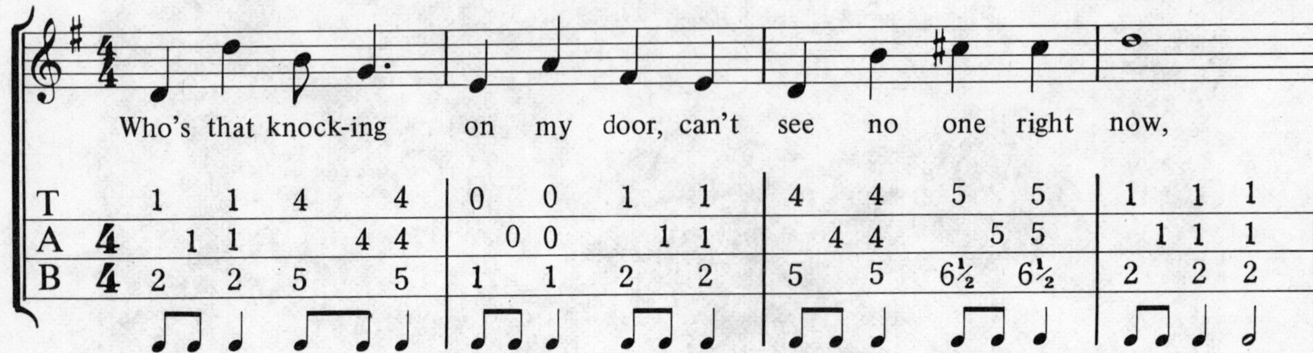


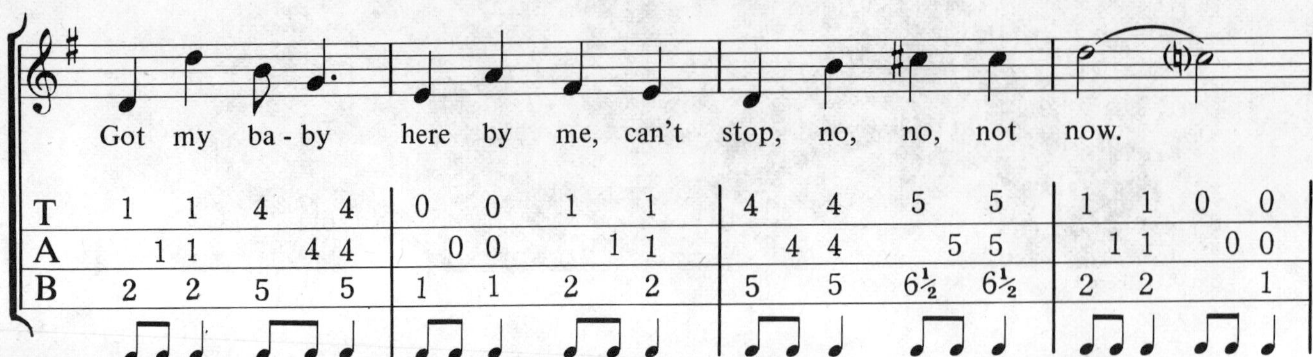

## Chorus

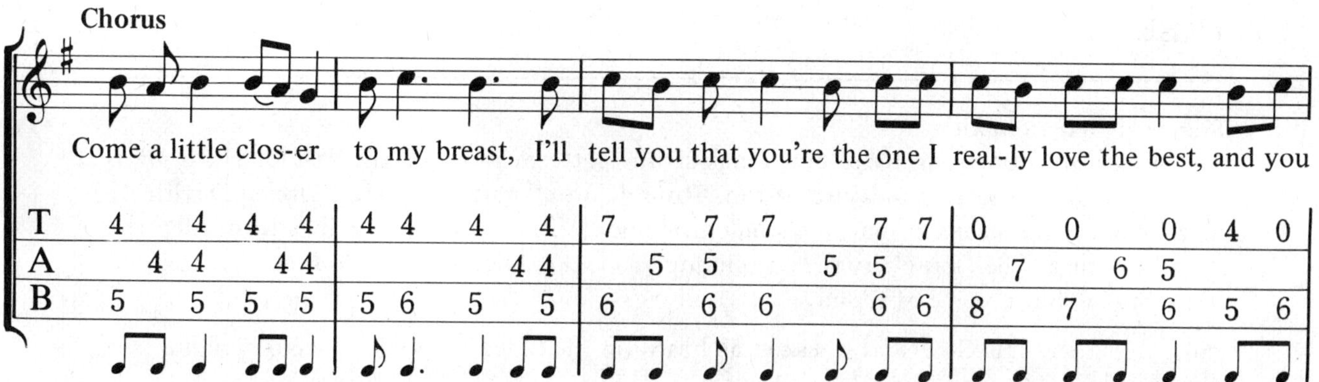


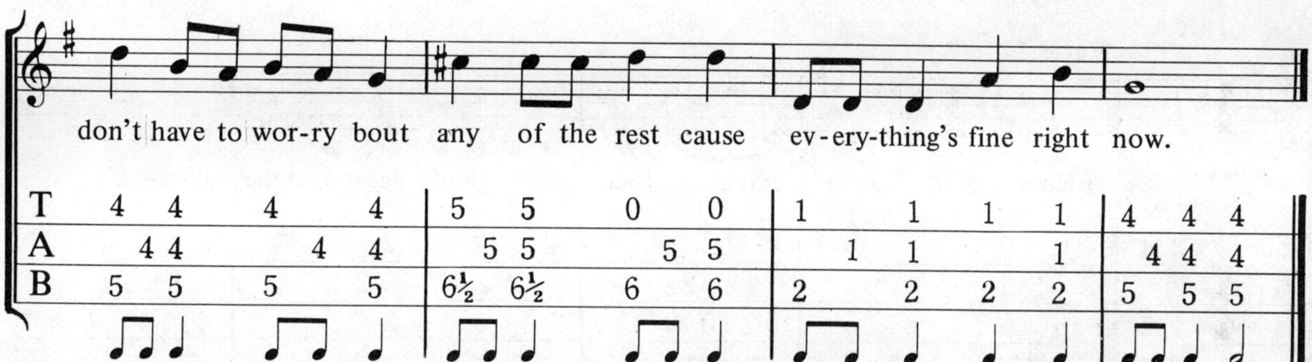


And you don't have to laugh,
and you don't have to sing,
You don't have to do nothing at all.
Just lay around and do as you please,
You haven't got far to fa-all.

**Chorus:**
Come a little closer to my breast,
I'll tell you that you're the one
I really love the best,
And you don't have to worry 'bout
any of the rest,
Cause everything's fine right now.

Oh my, my it looks kind of dark,
Looks like the clouds rolled on.
Best thing you could do is just stay here with me
At least just until da-awn.
**Chorus:**

## TREE

Standard Lydian Mode

The *verses* are done in a basic pinch-pick-strum pattern. Most of the rest of the song is strummed. In the second measure of the "Rum-de-dum" part you'll see a circled D with x's in the tab. This means to put one's index or middle finger over the strings to deaden the sound, so that, when struck by the strumming hand, the dulcimer will produce a percussion-like' 'chuka-chuka" type of sound.

Tune dulcimer: DD-G-C. This song can be heard on the "Pied Pumpkins" second album (see discography).

Words and music
by Rick Scott

Have no fear of falling down,
That's the way you go. The Old One told me.
Now I hear a painful sound,
I wish that there was someone to hold me.
    But if you need the miracle of my grain
    To keep the water off your head,
    Just remember, your life and mine
        are the same.

**Bridge** *(after 2nd verse.)*

| 4/4 | | | |
|---|---|---|---|
| 5 5 5 4 4 3 3 2 2 | 3 4 5 5 5 4 4 | 3 0 0 |
| 6 6 6 5 5 4 4 3 3 | 4 5 6 6 6 5 5 | 4 7 7 |
| 0 0 0 0 0 0 0 0 0 | 0 0 0 0 0 0 0 | 0 0 0 |

| | | |
|---|---|---|
| 0 0 3 3 4 4 5 0 | 0 0 3 3 4 4 5 0 | 0 0 3 3 4 4 3 3 |
| 7 7 4 4 5 5 6 8 | 7 7 4 4 5 5 6 8 | 7 7 4 4 5 5 4 4 |
| 0 0 0 0 0 0 0 0 | 0 0 0 0 0 0 0 0 | 0 0 0 0 0 0 0 0 |

*(repeat twice)*

| | | | |
|---|---|---|---|
| 2 2 1 1 0 2 3 | 4 4 4 5 4 3 2 3 | 4 4 4 5 4 3 3 | 0 |
| 3 3 1 1 0 0 0 | 0 0 0 0 0 0 0 0 | 0 0 0 0 0 0 0 | 5 |
| 0 0 0 0 0 0 0 | 0 0 0 0 0 0 0 0 | 0 0 0 0 0 0 0 | 6 |

*Repeat 2nd verse and Bridge.*

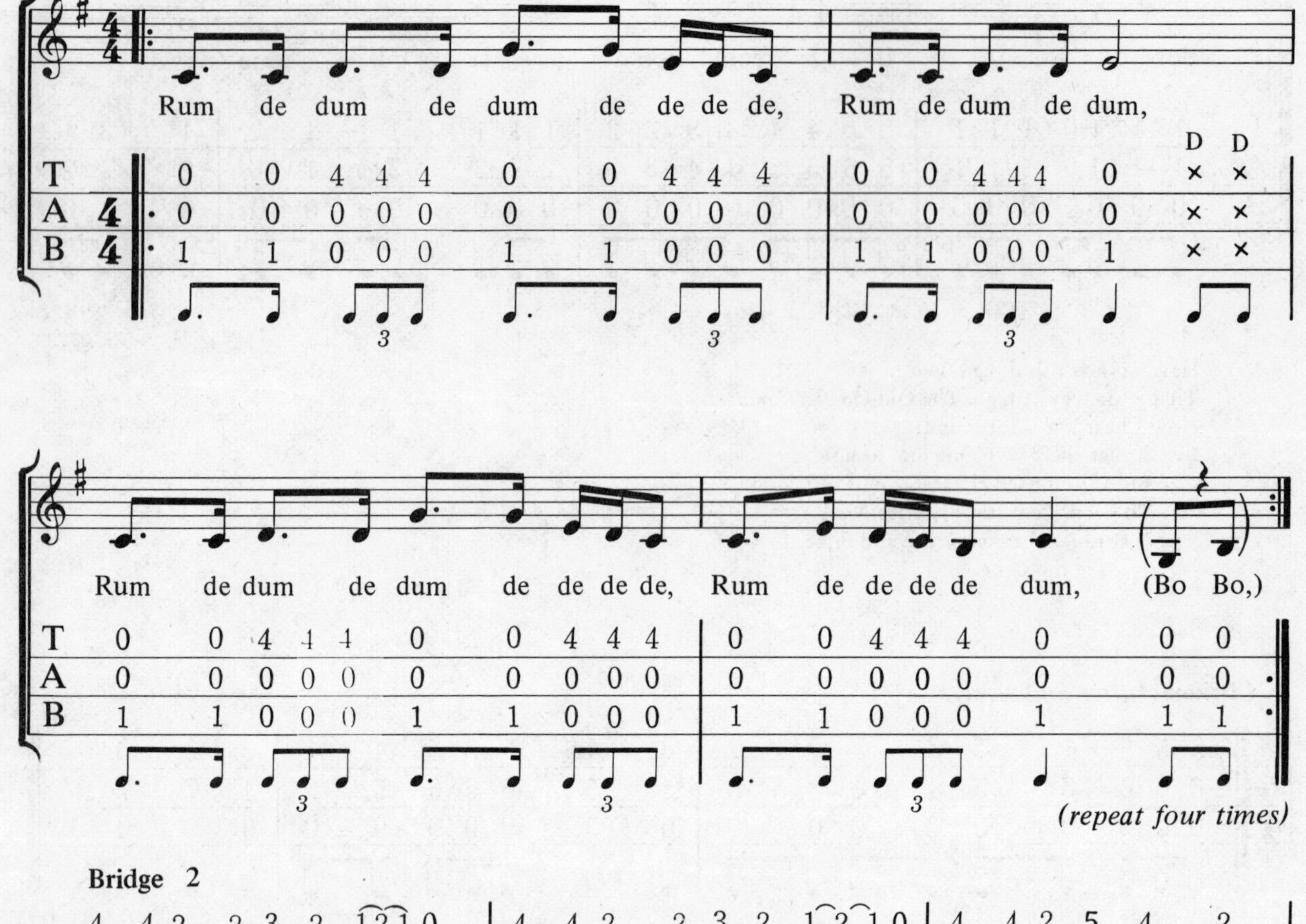


**Bridge 2**

```
4  4 2  2 3 2  1 2 1 0 | 4  4 2  2 3 2  1 2 1 0 | 4  4 2 5  4  2
0  0 0  0 0 0  0 0 0 0 | 0  0 0  0 0 0  0 0 0 0 | 0  0 0 0  0  0
0  0 0  0 0 0  0 0 0 0 | 0  0 0  0 0 0  0 0 0 0 | 0  0 0 0  0  0
```

```
3 3 3  3  2 1 0 | 4  4 2  2 3  3 2 1 | 0  0  1 2 1  0
0 0 0  0  0 0 0 | 0  0 0  0 0  0 0 0 | 0  0  0 0 0  0
0 0 0  0  0 0 0 | 0  0 0  0 0  0 0 0 | 0  0  0 0 0  0
```

*Repeat part B ("Rum De Dum" section and Bridge 2 ) this time repeating the "Rum De Dum" parts three times.*

## MINUET

Tune your dulcimer to GG-E-C (Ionian Mode of C).

Traditional
Arranged by Daron Douglas

```
3/4
|          |      4 | 3 1    | 2      | 0      |      4 | 3 1    |   |
| 0 0 3    | 2      | 0      | 2 1 0  | 0      | 2      | 0      | 2 |
|          | 2 2 5  | 1   2  |        |      3 | 2  2 5 | 1   2  | 2 |

| 0        | 4 5    | 7          | 4 4 5 4 | 0      | 3 4    | 3 4 3        | 2 0 |
|     0    |     4  |            |   1 4   |        |      3 |              |     |
| 5 6 7    | 4      | 5 6 5 4 3  | 4       | 5 6 7  | 1 2 3  | 4 3 232 3    | 3   |

|          |      4 | 3 1    | 2      | 0      |      4 | 3 2 1        | 5 |
| 0 0 3    | 2      | 0      | 2 1 0  |  0 3   | 2      |              | 5 |
|          | 2 2 5  | 1   2  |        |        | 2  2 5 | 2 232 2      | 5 |
```



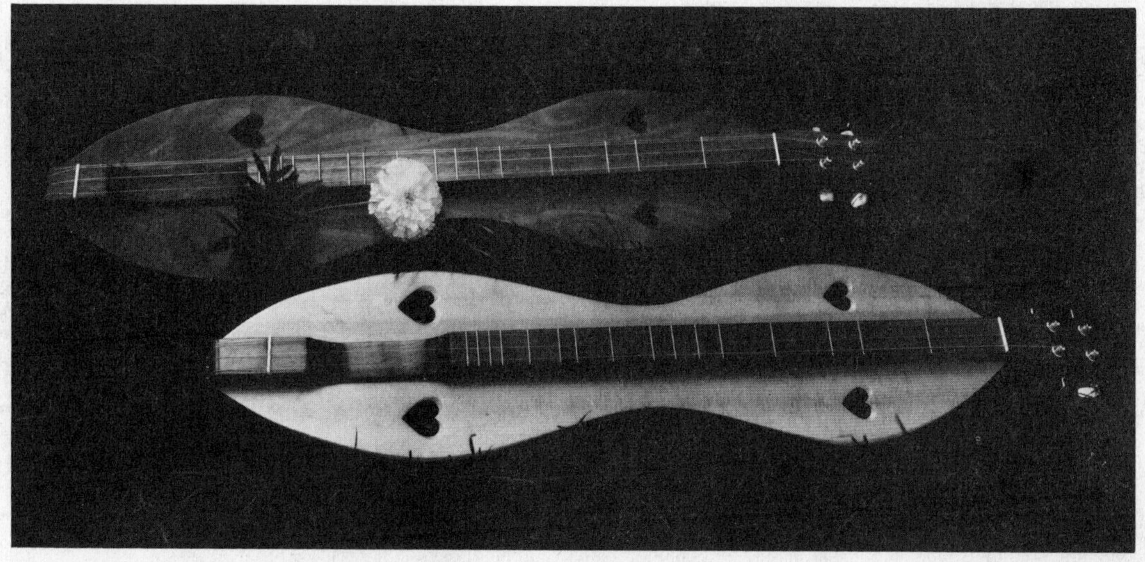

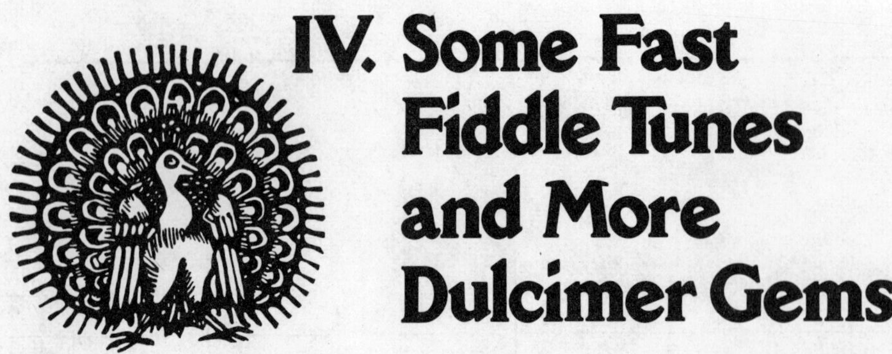

# IV. Some Fast Fiddle Tunes and More Dulcimer Gems

## IRISH WASHERWOMAN–DROP OF WHISKEY (Medley)

Fretting with your fingers would be better than using a noter for this medley. You can use any standard Mixolydian tuning. Try DD-A-D, since these tunes are traditionally done in the key of D.

Traditional
In the style of Walker Fanning

**Irish Washerwoman**
**Part A**

| 6/8 | | | | | | | | | |
|---|---|---|---|---|---|---|---|---|---|
| | 0 0 | 000000 | 000000 | 000000 | 000000 | 000000 | 000000 | 000000 | 0000 |
| | 0 0 | 000000 | 000000 | 000000 | 000000 | 000000 | 000000 | 000000 | 0000 |
| | 4 3 | 200000 | 202432 | 311111 | 313543 | 200000 | 202432 | 323143 | 2000 |

**Part B**

| | | | | | | | | |
|---|---|---|---|---|---|---|---|---|
| 0 0 | 000000 | 000000 | 000 000 | 000000 | 000000 | 0000 0 | 000000 | 0000 |
| 0 0 | 000000 | 000000 | 000 000 | 000000 | 000000 | 0000 0 | 000000 | 0000 |
| 7 8 | 977477 | 979987 | 86½6½46½6½ | 86½8 8 76½ | 577477 | 3772 2 | 323143 | 2000 |

**Drop of Whiskey**
**Part A**

| | | | | | |
|---|---|---|---|---|---|
| 0 0 | 000000 | 0 0000 | 0 00 0 | 000000 | 000000 |
| 0 0 | 000000 | 0 0000 | 0 00 0 | 000000 | 000000 |
| 4 3 | 202202 | 4 3202 | 3 14 3 | 202202 | 454202 |

| 0 0 0 0 0 0 | 0 0 0 0 | 0 0 0 0 0 | 0 0 0 0 0 0 | 0 0 0 0 0 | 0 0 |
|---|---|---|---|---|---|
| 0 0 0 0 0 0 | 0 0 0 0 | 0 0 0 0 0 | 0 0 0 0 0 0 | 0 0 0 0 0 | 0 0 |
| 2 0 2 3 2 3 | 1 1 3 1 | 4 3 2 0 2 | 2 0 2 3 2 3 | 1 1 3 2 1 | 0 0 |

**Part B**

| 0 0 | 0 0 0 0 0 | 0 0 0 0 | 0 0 0 0 0 0 | 0 0 0 0 0 | 0 0 0 0 0 | 0 0 0 0 0 | 0 0 0 0 0 | 0 0 0 0 |
|---|---|---|---|---|---|---|---|---|
| 0 0 | 0 0 0 0 0 | 0 0 0 0 | 0 0 0 0 0 0 | 0 0 0 0 0 | 0 0 0 0 0 | 0 0 0 0 0 | 0 0 0 0 0 | 0 0 0 0 |
| 0 0 | 0 2 4 7 4 | 2 4 7 4 | 0 2 4 5 4 2 | 3 2 3 1 1 | 0 2 4 7 7 | 9 8 7 4 2 | 3 2 3 1 1 | 3 2 1 0 |

Philadelphia Folk Festival

## OVER THE WATERFALL
(Two Versions)

The first version is composed for a dulcimer with the "extra" fret between the 6th and 7th frets. It is written for either Mixolydian tuning, while the second is for the standard Mixolydian (DD-A-D). One may of course add chords to either version or play none at all. I like to fret both versions with my fingers instead of a noter. Traditionally played in the key of D.

Traditional
Arranged by Neal and Sally Hellman

**Version I**
**Part A**

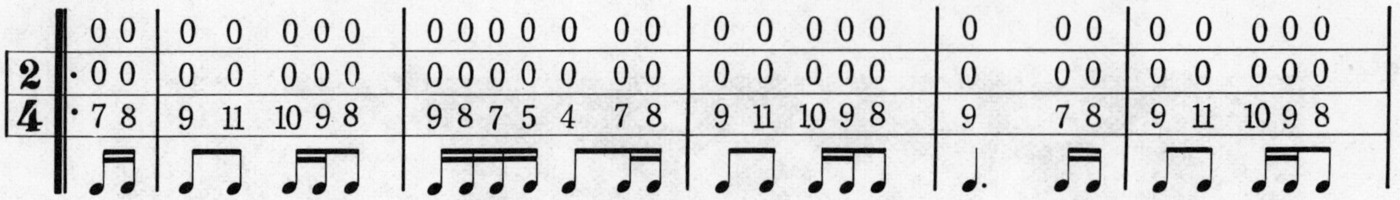

2/4

| | | | | | |
|---|---|---|---|---|---|
| 0 0 | 0 0 0 0 0 | 0 0 0 0 0 0 0 | 0 0 0 0 0 | 0 0 0 | 0 0 0 0 0 |
| 0 0 | 0 0 0 0 0 | 0 0 0 0 0 0 0 | 0 0 0 0 0 | 0 0 0 | 0 0 0 0 0 |
| 7 8 | 9 11 10 9 8 | 9 8 7 5 4 7 8 | 9 11 10 9 8 | 9 7 8 | 9 11 10 9 8 |

**Part B**

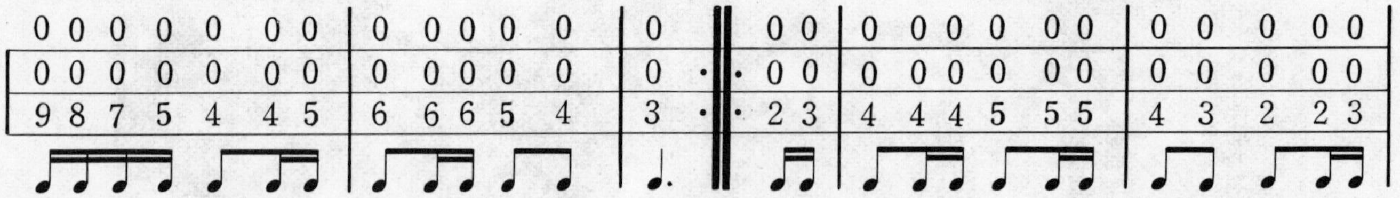

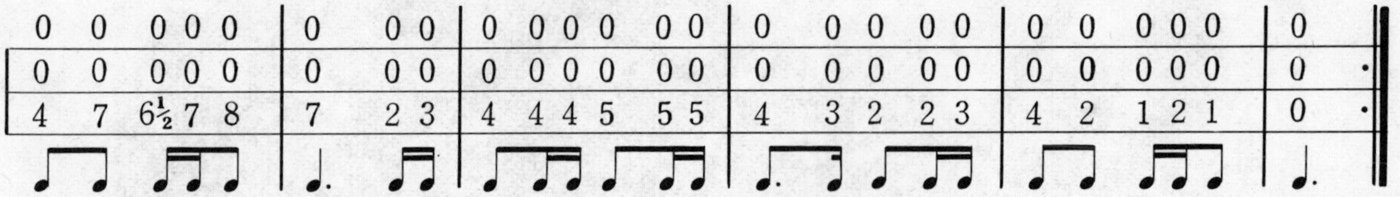

| | | | | | |
|---|---|---|---|---|---|
| 0 0 0 0 0 0 0 | 0 0 0 0 0 | 0 | 0 0 | 0 0 0 0 0 0 | 0 0 0 0 0 |
| 0 0 0 0 0 0 0 | 0 0 0 0 0 | 0 | 0 0 | 0 0 0 0 0 0 | 0 0 0 0 0 |
| 9 8 7 5 4 4 5 | 6 6 6 5 4 | 3 | 2 3 | 4 4 4 5 5 5 | 4 3 2 2 3 |

| | | | | | |
|---|---|---|---|---|---|
| 0 0 0 0 0 | 0 0 0 | 0 0 0 0 0 0 | 0 0 0 0 0 | 0 0 0 0 0 | 0 |
| 0 0 0 0 0 | 0 0 0 | 0 0 0 0 0 0 | 0 0 0 0 0 | 0 0 0 0 0 | 0 |
| 4 7 6½ 7 8 | 7 2 3 | 4 4 4 5 5 5 | 4 3 2 2 3 | 4 2 1 2 1 | 0 |

**Version II**

**Part A**

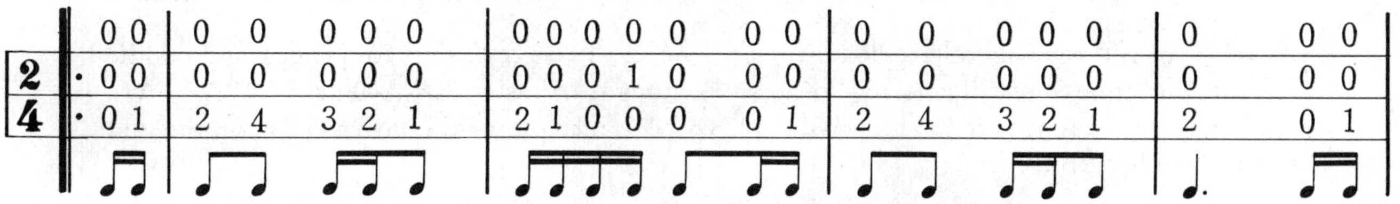

```
2/4
|: 0 0 | 0 0  0 0 0 | 0 0 0 0 0  0 0 | 0 0  0 0 0 | 0  0 0 |
|: 0 0 | 0 0  0 0 0 | 0 0 0 1 0  0 0 | 0 0  0 0 0 | 0  0 0 |
|: 0 1 | 2 4  3 2 1 | 2 1 0 0 0  0 1 | 2 4  3 2 1 | 2  0 1 |
```

**Part B**

```
| 0 0  0 0 0 | 0 0 0 0 0  0 0 | 6* 6 6 0  0 | 3*  ||  0 0 | 0  0 0 3  3 3 |
| 0 0  0 0 0 | 0 0 0 1 0  0 0 | 6  6 6 6  5 | 3  :||: 0 0 | 3  3 3 3  3 3 |
| 2 4  3 2 1 | 2 1 0 0 0  0 0 | 6  6 6 5  4 | 3  :||: 2 3 | 4  4 4 5  5 5 |
```

```
| 0 0  0 0 0 | 0 0  0 0 0 | 0  0 0 | 0 0 0 3  3 3 | 0  0 0  0 0 | 0 0  0 0 0 | 0  ||
| 3 0  0 0 0 | 0 3  2 3 4 | 3  0 0 | 3 3 3 3  3 3 | 3  0 0  0 0 | 0 0  0 0 0 | 0 :||
| 4 3  2 2 3 | 4 0  0 0 0 | 0  2 2 | 4 4 4 5  5 5 | 4  3 2  2 3 | 4 2  1 2 1 | 0 :||
```



*Can be played as barre chords.

## FISHER'S HORNPIPE

Any Ionian tuning will do here. Play it with a noter or else try using your index and middle fingers. The tune is usually played in D, so you might try using AA-A-D or AA-D-A or AA-D-D. You can play it in the D Mixolydian (DD-A-D) but you would have to start on the 2nd fret and take it from there.

Traditional
In the style of Bonnie Russell

**Part A**

```
    | 0 | 0 0 0 0 0  0 0 | 0  0 0 0  0 0 | 0 0 0 0 0  0 0 | 0 0 0  |
4/4 | 0 | 0 0 0 0 0  0 0 | 0  0 0 0  0 0 | 0 0 0 0 0  0 0 | 0 0 0  |
    | 5 | 10 5 6 7 5 6 7 | 5  6 7 5  4 9 | 10 5 6 7 5 6 7 | 5 9 10 |
```

**Part B**

```
| 0 | 0 0 0 0  0 0 0 0     | 0 0 0 0 0 0 0      | 0 0 0 0  0 0 0 0 | 0 0 0 0 |
| 0 | 0 0 0 0  0 0 0 0     | 0 0 0 0 0 0 0      | 0 0 0 0  0 0 0 0 | 0 0 0 0 |
| 9 | 11 9 11 9 11 12 11 9 | 11 9 11 12 10 8 7  | 8 6 5 6  7 5 4 5 | 7 5 4 3 |
```

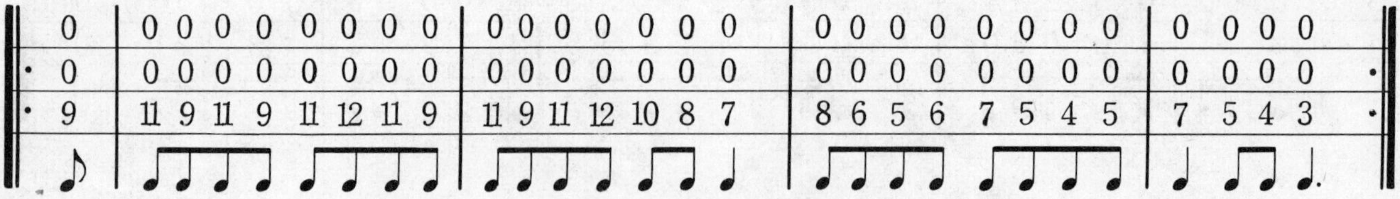

## EBENEZER

Use any Ionian tuning: AA-A-D or AA-D-D or DD-G-D, etc. This should be played very fast using your fingers or a noter.

Traditional
In the style of Bonnie Russell

**Part A**

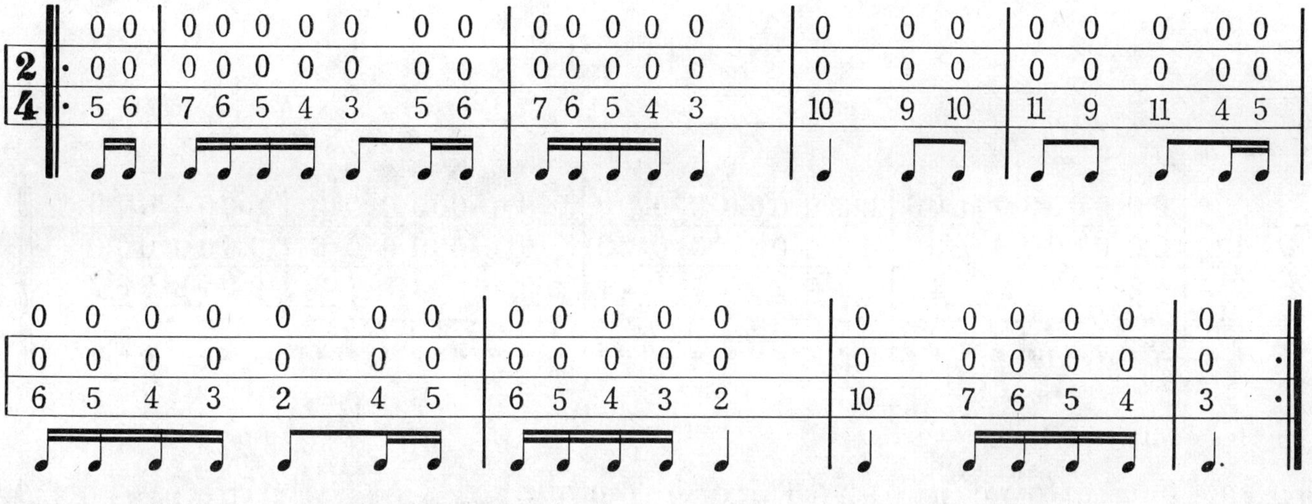

```
    |: 0 0 | 0 0 0 0 0   0 0 | 0 0 0 0 0 | 0    0 0 | 0  0  0   0 0 |
 2  |: 0 0 | 0 0 0 0 0   0 0 | 0 0 0 0 0 | 0    0 0 | 0  0  0   0 0 |
 4  |: 5 6 | 7 6 5 4 3   5 6 | 7 6 5 4 3 | 10   9 10| 11 9  11  4 5 |
```

```
| 0 0 0 0 0   0 0 | 0 0 0 0 0 | 0    0 0 0 0 | 0  ||
| 0 0 0 0 0   0 0 | 0 0 0 0 0 | 0    0 0 0 0 | 0 :||
| 6 5 4 3 2   4 5 | 6 5 4 3 2 | 10   7 6 5 4 | 3 :||
```

**Part B**

```
|: 0 0 | 0    0 0 0  0  | 0  0  0  0 0 | 0    0 0 0  0  |
|: 0 0 | 0    0 0 0  0  | 0  0  0  0 0 | 0    0 0 0  0  |
|: 8 9 | 10   8 9 10 11 | 12 11 12 8 9 | 10   8 9 10 11 |
```

```
| 0  0  0  0  0  | 0  0  0  0 0  | 0  0 0  0 | 0    0 0 0 0 | 0  ||
| 0  0  0  0  0  | 0  0  0  0 0  | 0  0 0  0 | 0    0 0 0 0 | 0 :||
| 12 11 12 10 11 | 12 11 12 9 10 | 11 9 11 9 | 10   7 6 5 4 | 3 :||
```

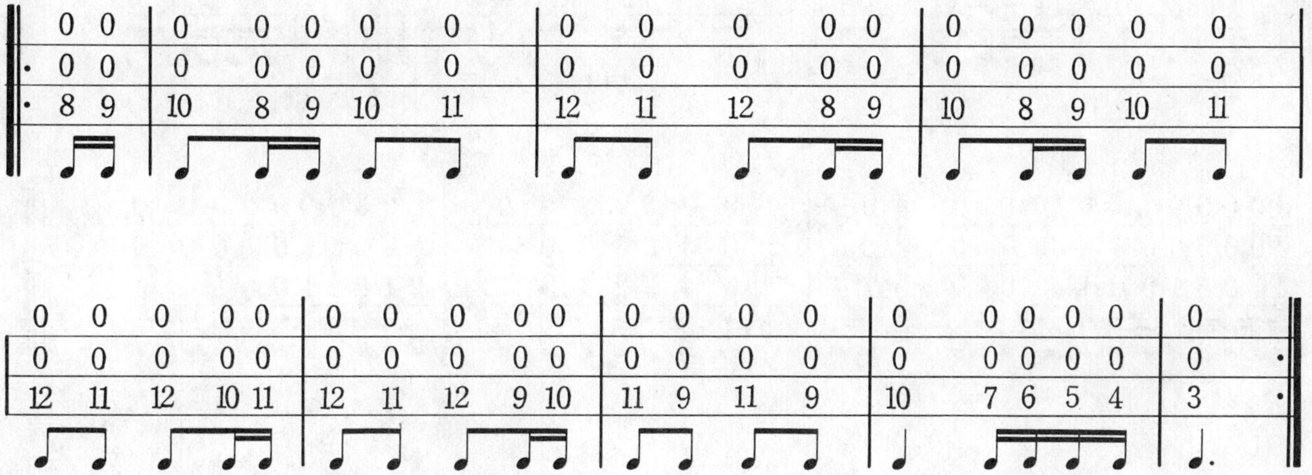

## SOLDIER'S JOY

Standard Mixolydian DD-A-D (this tune is usually played in D) Try using the following fretting method instead of a noter.

Station your thumb over the 4th fret and your index finger over the 2nd. Any fret above and including the 4th will be played by sliding the side of your thumb, and any fret below the 4th (including those on the middle string) will be played by the top of your index finger. Try doing some hammer-ons and pull-offs; you'll see the advantage your fingers have over using a noter.

Traditional
In the style of Kevin Roth

**Part A**

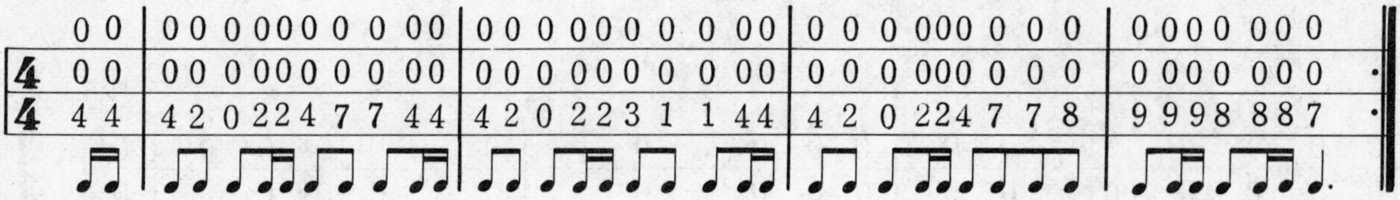

```
    0 0 | 00 0 000 0 0 0 00 | 0 0 0 000 0 0 0 00 | 0 0 0 000 0 0 0 | 0000 000  ||
4   0 0 | 00 0 000 0 0 0 00 | 0 0 0 000 0 0 0 00 | 0 0 0 000 0 0 0 | 0000 000 :||
4   4 4 | 4 2 0 224 7 7 4 4 | 4 2 0 223 1 1 4 4  | 4 2 0 224 7 7 8 | 9998 887 :||
```

**Part B**

```
||  00 | 0 0 0 000 0 0 00 | 0 0 0 000 0 0 00 | 0 0 0 000 0 0 0
||: 00 | 0 0 0 000 0 0 00 | 0 0 0 000 1 0 00 | 0 0 0 000 0 0 0
||: 00 | 0 2 4 221 2 3 21 | 0 2 4 221 0 0 00 | 0 2 4 221 2 3

000000000 0 0 0  || 00 | 0 0 0 000 0 0 | 000000000 0 0 ||
000000100 0 0 0 :|| 00 | 0 0 0 000 0 0 | 000000100 0 0 ||
210210010 0 0 0 :|| 77 | 7 5 4 223 5 4 | 210210010 0 0 ||
```

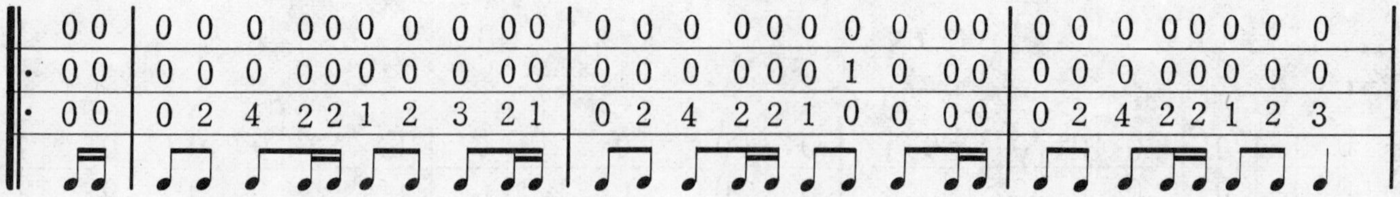

## CHILD GROVE

Since the melody is played on the first string any Aeolian tuning can be utilized. Try CC-A-D (Dm), GG-A-E (Am), or any others you wish.

Traditional
Arranged by Neal and Sally Hellman

**Part A**

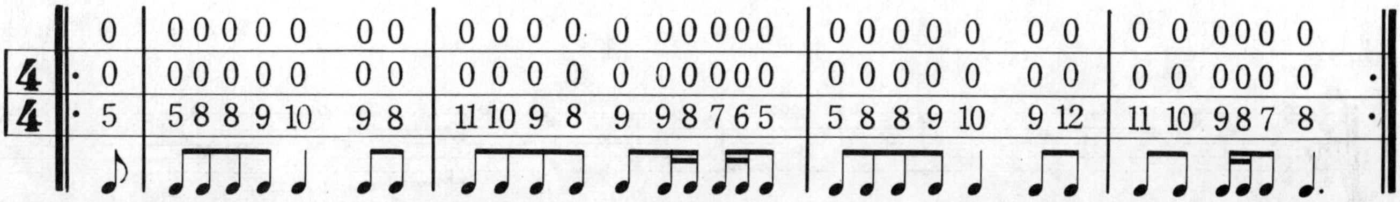

| | | | | |
|---|---|---|---|---|
| 0 | 0 0 0 0 0 0 0 | 0 0 0 0 0 0 0 0 0 0 | 0 0 0 0 0 0 0 | 0 0 0 0 0 0 |
| 0 | 0 0 0 0 0 0 0 | 0 0 0 0 0 0 0 0 0 0 | 0 0 0 0 0 0 0 | 0 0 0 0 0 0 |
| 5 | 5 8 8 9 10 9 8 | 11 10 9 8 9 9 8 7 6 5 | 5 8 8 9 10 9 12 | 11 10 9 8 7 8 |

**Part B**

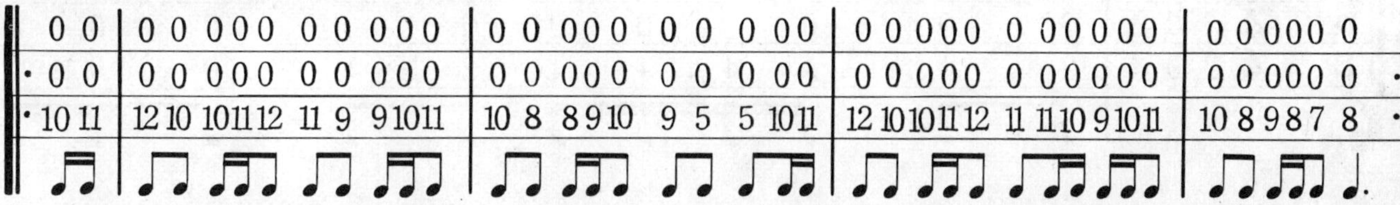

| | | | | |
|---|---|---|---|---|
| 0 0 | 0 0 0 0 0 0 0 0 0 0 | 0 0 0 0 0 0 0 0 0 0 | 0 0 0 0 0 0 0 0 0 0 0 | 0 0 0 0 0 0 |
| 0 0 | 0 0 0 0 0 0 0 0 0 0 | 0 0 0 0 0 0 0 0 0 0 | 0 0 0 0 0 0 0 0 0 0 0 | 0 0 0 0 0 0 |
| 10 11 | 12 10 10 11 12 11 9 9 10 11 | 10 8 8 9 10 9 5 5 10 11 | 12 10 10 11 12 11 11 10 9 10 11 | 10 8 9 8 7 8 |



## JUNE APPLE

Use any New Mixolydian tuning (try AA-E-E since this is played a lot in A). All bass notes are fretted with the index finger. All notes below the 7th fret on the melody string are played by the middle finger. However, the 5th fret in the first and third bars should be played by the thumb as it slides down from the 7th fret. This is usually played in A or G.

Traditional
In the style of John Prisland

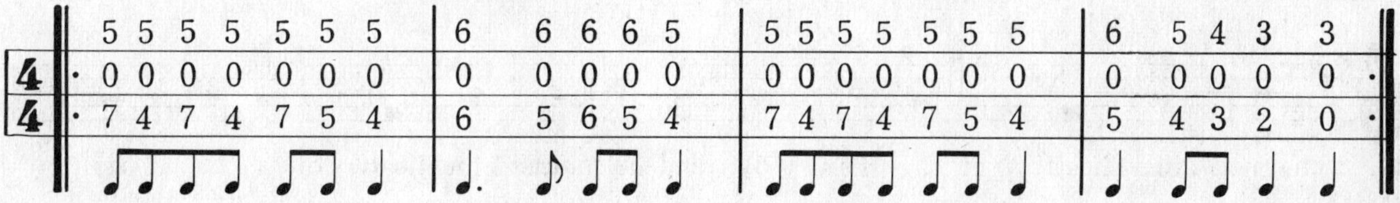

| | | | |
|---|---|---|---|
| 5 5 5 5 5 5 5 | 6 6 6 6 5 | 5 5 5 5 5 5 5 | 6 5 4 3 3 |
| 0 0 0 0 0 0 0 | 0 0 0 0 0 | 0 0 0 0 0 0 0 | 0 0 0 0 0 |
| 7 4 7 4 7 5 4 | 6 5 6 5 4 | 7 4 7 4 7 5 4 | 5 4 3 2 0 |

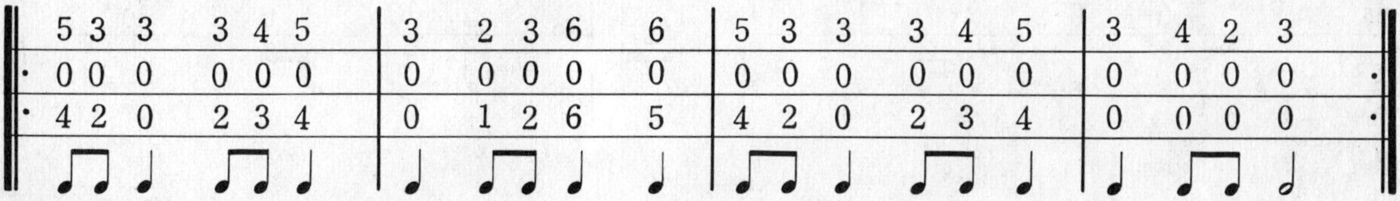

| | | | |
|---|---|---|---|
| 5 3 3 3 4 5 | 3 2 3 6 6 | 5 3 3 3 4 5 | 3 4 2 3 |
| 0 0 0 0 0 0 | 0 0 0 0 0 | 0 0 0 0 0 0 | 0 0 0 0 |
| 4 2 0 2 3 4 | 0 1 2 6 5 | 4 2 0 2 3 4 | 0 0 0 0 |

## BLACK JACK DAVY

Tune to AA-A-E, which is a "new" Mixolydian tuning of A. If you use the standard Mixolydian of (AA-E-A) be sure to reverse the middle and bass strings of the dulcimer tab. The chords are made with the middle finger on the melody strings and the index finger on the bass. The phrase "and he charmed the heart of a lady" is best done with the index finger only.

Traditional
In the style of Kevin Roth

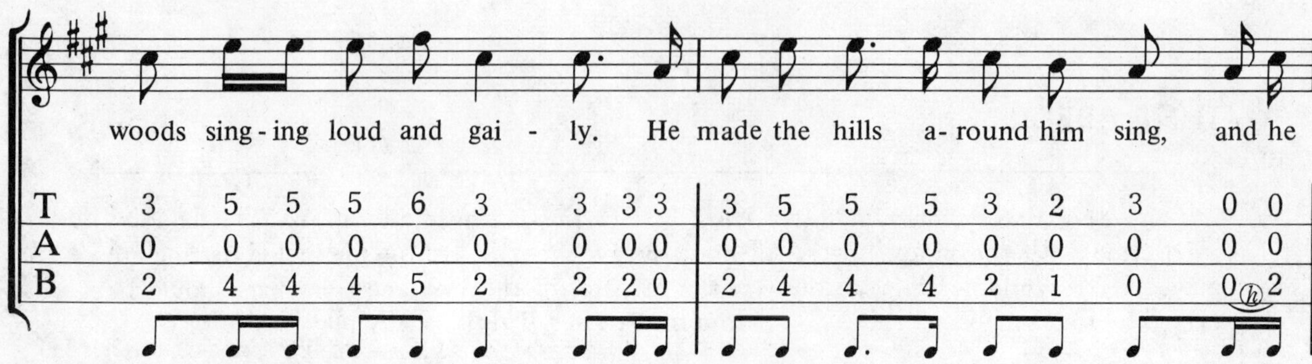

How old are you my pretty little miss?
How old are you my honey?
She answered him with a silly little grin
I'll be sixteen next Sunday. *(2x)*

Come away with me my pretty little miss,
Come away with me my honey,
I'll take you cross the deep blue sea
Where you'll never need for money. *(2x)*

She kicked off her high heel boots,
All made of Spanish leather,
And she put on her low heel shoes
And they rode off together. *(2x)*

My lord came home late last night,
inquiring for his lady;
The servant spoke before he thought,
She's gone with Black Jack Davy. *(2x)*

Go saddle up my milk white steed,
Saddle her slow and easy,
I'll ride all night 'til broad daylight,
And I'll overtake my lady. *(2x)*

Well he rode all day and he rode all night
Till he came to the edge of the water,
And there he saw his own true love,
At the side of the Black Jack Davy. *(2x)*

Will you forsake your house and home?
Your husband and your lady's?
Will you forsake your new born babe?
To ride with Gypsy Davy? *(2x)*

Yes I'll forsake my house and home,
My husband and my lady's.
And I'll forsake my new born babe
To ride with the Gypsy Davy. *(2x)*

Last nite she slept in a feather bed
With her husband and baby,
Tonight she'll sleep on the cold clay ground
At the side of the Gypsy Davy. *(2x)*

Shilo Hellman

## THE FLOWERS OF THE FOREST

This one is in D Mixolydian. Tune dulcimer DD-A-D, DD-D-D or DD-D-A.

Traditional
Arranged by Neal and Sally Hellman

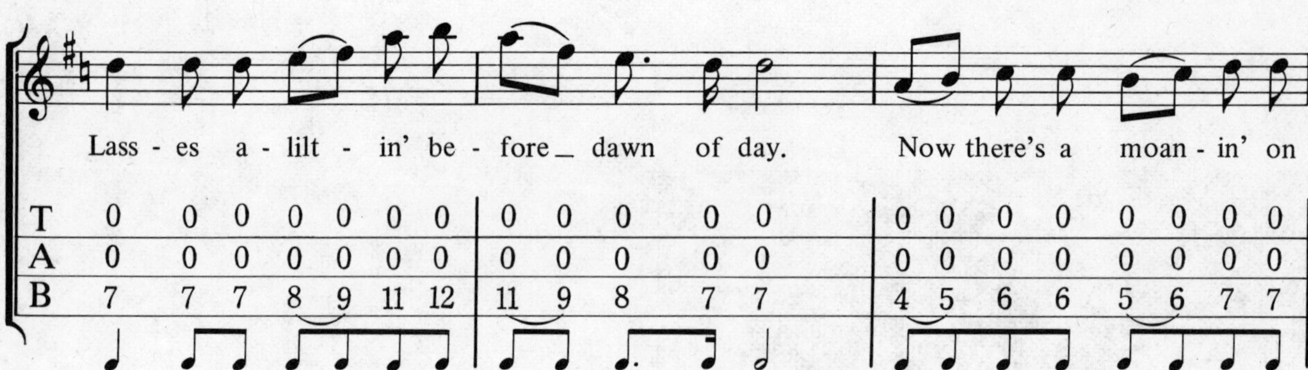


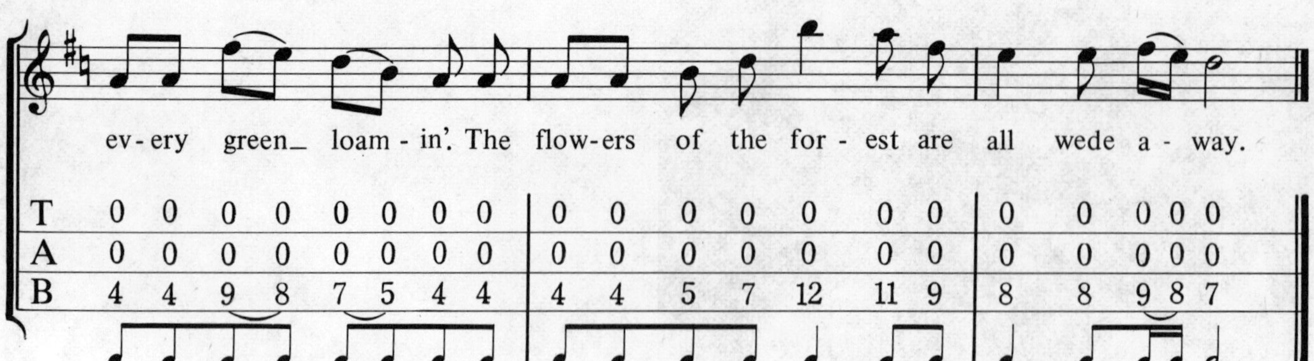

At bughts in the mornin',
nae blithe lads are scornin',
Lasses are lonely and dowie and wae;
Nae daffin' nae gabbin', but sighin' and sabbin';
Ilk ane lifts her leglin and hies her away.

At e'en in the gloamin'
nae swankies are roamin'
Bout stacks wi' the lasses at bogle to play;
But ilk maid sits drearie,
lamentin' her dearie.
The Flowers of the Forest are a'wede away.

In har'st at the shearin',
nae youths now are jeerin';
Bandsters are runkled and lyart and grey;
At fair or at preachin'
nae wooin' nae fleechin',
The Flowers of the Forest are all wede away.

Dool for the order that sent
our lads to the border,
The English for ance by guile wan the say.
The Flower of the Forest that
fought aye the foremost
The prime of our land lies cold in the clay.

We'll hae nae mair liltin'
at the ewe milkin',
Women and bairns are heartless and wae;
Sighin' and moanin' on ilka green loanin',
The Flowers of the Forest
are all wede away.

## A MAID THAT'S DEEP IN LOVE

This is written out for the A Mixolydian Mode. Tune it AA-E-A, AA-A-E or AA-A-A. All three, of course, are Mixolydian tunings of A. This song sounds nice with a noter.

Traditional
Arranged by Neal and Sally Hellman

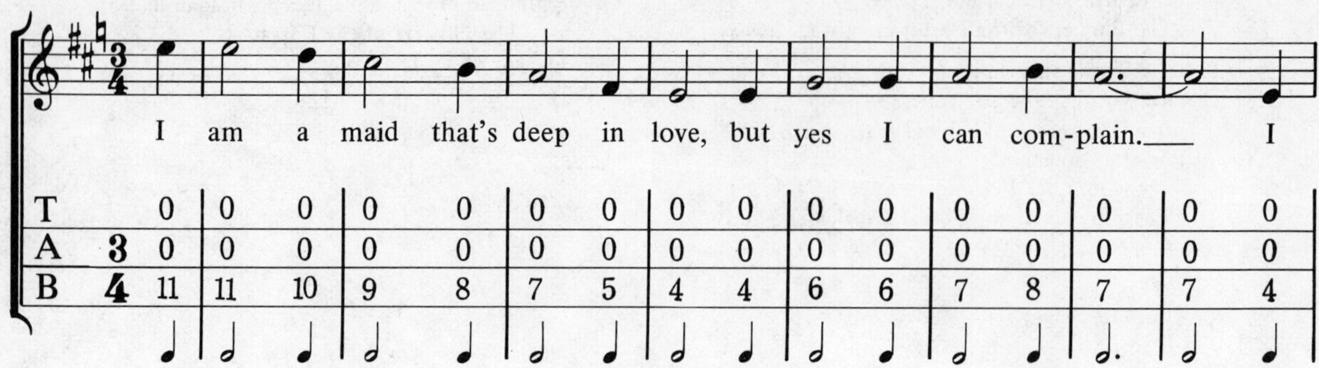


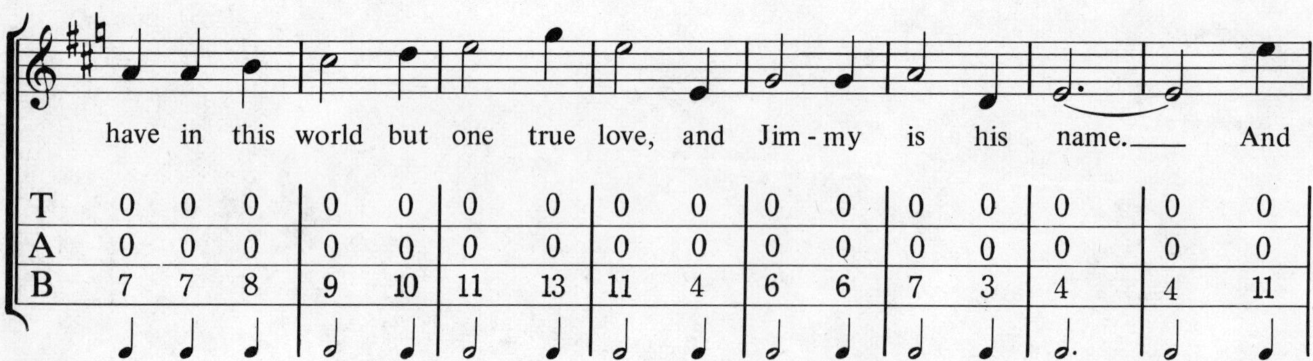

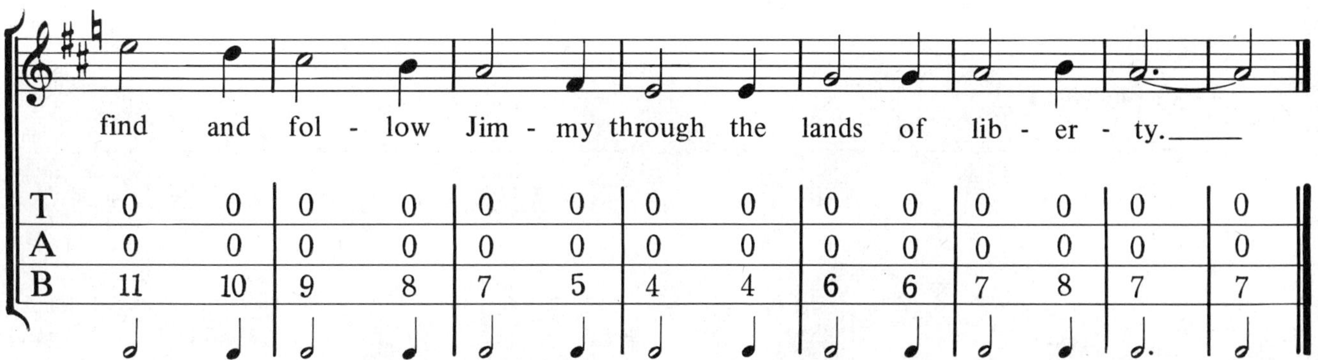


Then I'll put up my yellow hair,
Men's clothing I'll wear on,
I'll sign to a bold sea captain,
My passage I'll work free,
And I'll find and follow Jimmy through
The Lands of liberty.

Then I'll put up my yellow hair,
Men's clothing I'll wear on,
I'll sign to a bold sea captain,
My passage I'll work free,
And I'll find and follow Jimmy through
The lands of liberty.
Farewell to my friends and all my kin,
A sailor I will be.

One night apon the raging sea
As we were a going to bed,
The captain cried farewell, my boy,
I wish you were a maid,
Your rosy cheeks, your ruby lips
They are enticing me,
And I wish, dear God, with all my heart
A maid you were to me.

Then hold your tongue, dear Captain,
Such talk is all in vain,
And if the sailors find it out
They'll laugh and make much game.
For when we reach Columbia shore
Some prettier girls you'll find,
And you'll laugh and sing and court with them
For courting you are inclined.

It was not three days after our ship
It reached the shore.
Adieu, my loving Captain,
Adieu for evermore.
For once I was a sailor on the sea,
But now I'm a maid on the shore.
So adieu to you and all your crew,
With you I'll sail no more.

Come back, come back, my own pretty maid,
Come back and marry me.
I have ten thousand pounds in gold
And that I give to thee.
So come back, come back, my own pretty maid,
Come back and marry me.

## SCOTLAND

Tune dulcimer to *any* standard Mixolydian tuning (DD-A-D, AA-A-E, etc.)

Traditional
Arranged by Nick Hallman

**Part I**

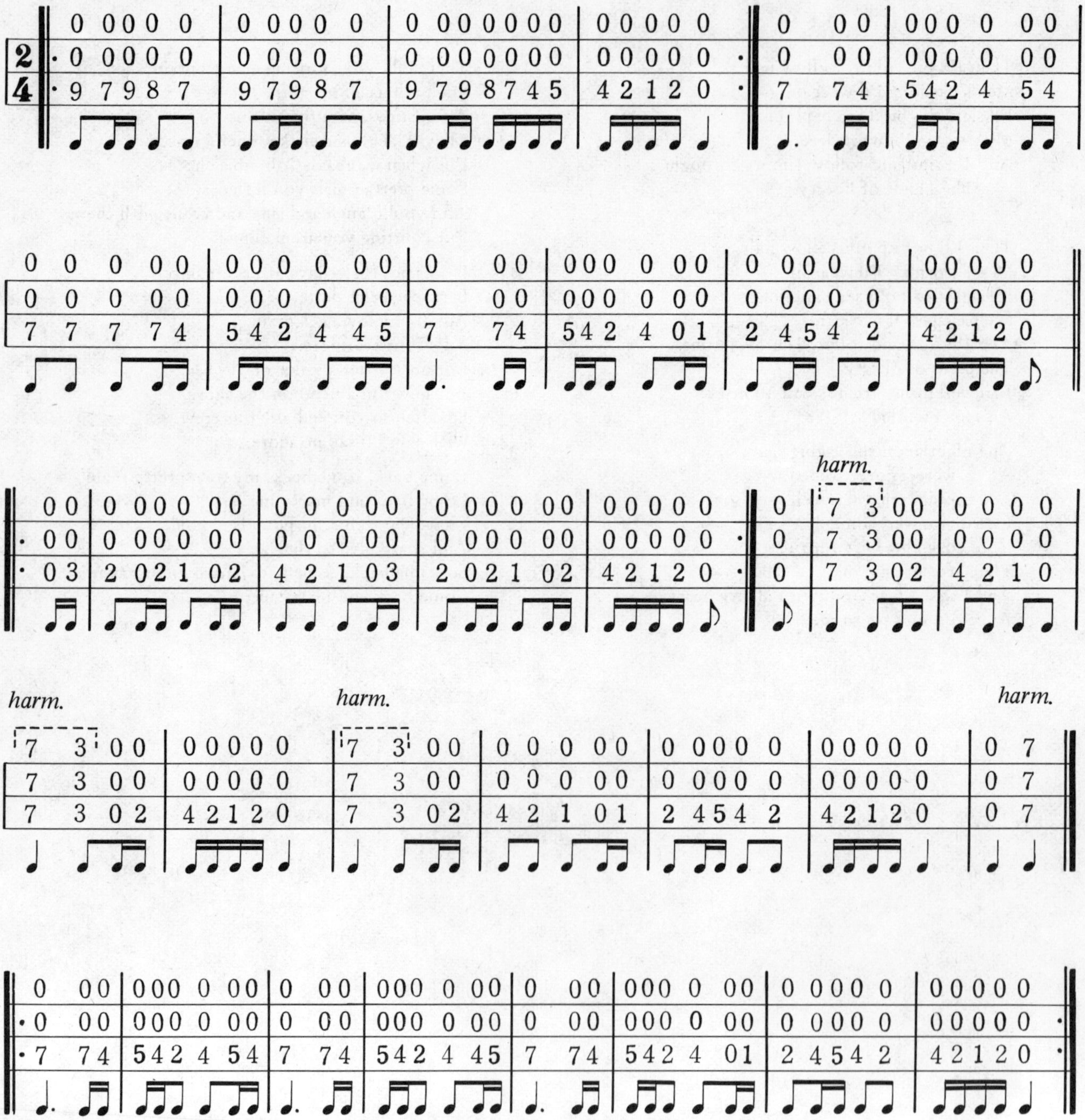

```
2/4
|| 0 000 0 | 0 000 0 | 0 000000  | 00000 || 0  00 | 000 0 00 |
|| 0 000 0 | 0 000 0 | 0 000000  | 00000 || 0  00 | 000 0 00 |
|| 9 798 7 | 9 798 7 | 9 798745  | 42120 || 7  74 | 542 4 54 |

 0 0 0 00 | 000 0 00 | 0  00 | 000 0 00 | 0 000 0 | 00000 ||
 0 0 0 00 | 000 0 00 | 0  00 | 000 0 00 | 0 000 0 | 00000 ||
 7 7 7 74 | 542 4 45 | 7  74 | 542 4 01 | 2 454 2 | 42120 ||

                                                   harm.
|| 00 | 0 000 00 | 0 0 0 00 | 0 000 00 | 00000 || 0 | 7 3 00 | 0000 |
|| 00 | 0 000 00 | 0 0 0 00 | 0 000 00 | 00000 || 0 | 7 3 00 | 0000 |
|| 03 | 2 021 02 | 4 2 1 03 | 2 021 02 | 42120 || 0 | 7 3 02 | 4210 |

harm.                 harm.                                      harm.
 7 3 00 | 00000 | 7 3 00 | 0 0 0 00 | 0 000 0 | 00000 | 0 7 ||
 7 3 00 | 00000 | 7 3 00 | 0 0 0 00 | 0 000 0 | 00000 | 0 7 ||
 7 3 02 | 42120 | 7 3 02 | 4 2 1 01 | 2 454 2 | 42120 | 0 7 ||

|| 0 00 | 000 0 00 | 0 00 | 000 0 00 | 0 00 | 000 0 00 | 0 000 0 | 00000 ||
|| 0 00 | 000 0 00 | 0 00 | 000 0 00 | 0 00 | 000 0 00 | 0 000 0 | 00000 ||
|| 7 74 | 542 4 54 | 7 74 | 542 4 45 | 7 74 | 542 4 01 | 2 454 2 | 42120 ||
```

# Appendices

## Appendix A: Modal Music

by Roger Nicholson

To the uninitiated listener the music of the East has an unusual and discordant quality; this is because it is based on an intricate modal system of various sharp, flat and natural notes interwoven with micro-tones which, while allowing an infinite variety of subtleties within the linear melodic form, contain much that is unfamiliar to ears accustomed to hearing music in a standard major or minor key, structured with layers of harmony and counterpoint. Also, Eastern music is mainly improvised, while the Western performer is only free to interpret matters of phrasing, tempo or dynamics and must play exactly what is written down. This, however, has not always been the case; up until the sixteenth century all European music was governed by a strict system of seven modes that, apart from plainchant, only survives today in the heritage of traditional music which also involves the use of variation and ornamentation.

Modes can be traced back to man's earliest civilizations in Assyria and Babylon where they were closely identified with astrology and astronomy. These people were very aware of the universal harmony of the universe, and concluded that as man could make music conforming to the same principles, he could become one with it. This philosophy is an integral part of Eastern music today, particularly in India where sounds are regarded as being of two types, those termed "unstruck" caused by the music of the spheres which can only be heard by the most advanced mystics, and "struck" sounds produced from musical instruments.

The Ancient Greeks (and, by tradition, Pythagoras) in the sixth century B.C. were the first to fix the modes scientifically, and did so by using the monochord—a single-stringed instrument with a fingerboard running along the top of a wooden soundbox on which the intervals were marked out—and named them after different races in Asia Minor. They are still so called and known as the Ionian, Dorian, Phrygian, Lydian, Mixolydian, Aeolian and Locrian modes. In addition, each was allotted its own character derived from aesthetic and astrological principles, so that the Ionian, Aeolian and Locrian were considered to have unsuitable aspects, while others such as the Lydian were recommended for their therapeutic properties.

In the early years of the Christian religion there was a strong Greek influence, and during the fourth century A.D. St. Ambrose, the Bishop of Milan, authorised the four original Greek modes (Dorian, Phrygian, Lydian and Mixolydian) for use in the church. To these "Authentic" modes, as they are known, Pope Gregory the Great (540-604) added four others known as "Plagal" modes which were really only other ways of utilizing the existing ones, but each began a fourth lower and were called the Hypo-Dorian, Hypo-Phrygian, etc., so establishing the form of plainchant which is still used today in the Roman Catholic church. These Plagal modes can also be played on the dulcimer; for example, tune to the Dorian but, instead of starting the scale at the fourth fret, begin on the first fret and continue up to the eighth.

For eleven hundred years modes dominated all forms of secular and religious music until gradually abandoned during the sixteenth century in favour of the major and minor scales, which were more suitable to the developing forms of harmony and counterpoint. In later years modes were occasionally used by some of the great composers, such as J.S. Bach in his "Dorian Toccata and Fugue," by

Mozart, whose Mass K.258(Missa Brevis in C major) is mainly Mixolydian, and Beethoven, who wrote one of the movements in his "String Quartet in A minor" in the Phrygian mode. During the late nineteenth century some English composers began to write modal works inspired by their discovery of traditional and early music, in particular Ralph Vaughan Williams, whose majestic "Fantasia on a Theme of Thomas Tallis" in the Phrygian mode is most well-known, and in France where Claude Debussy was directly influenced by the old European and Oriental modes in his piano works. Today the modes are beginning to be used again by Alan Hovhaness, an American of Armenian descent, Toru Takemitsu from Japan, and many others who are realising their potential in contemporary music.

A mode is not a key but an arrangement of the seven tones and semi-tones of a diatonic scale, and can be played at any pitch, so there are seven modes for each of the twelve keys. Below, for the sake of convenience in comparing them, they are all related to the key of C:

The *Ionian Mode* of C,D,E,F,G,A,B,C is the same as our modern Major scale; the Greek and Medieval theorists considered it to have extrovert and playful aspects, and so excluded it from use in the church–virtually the sole province of music at that time. Today music in this mode can still be considered to be bright or happy, as opposed to that in the minor, which tends to reflect sadness, and interesting comparisons can be drawn with the early morning Indian raga *Bilawai* which has identical intervals and is associated with light and happiness. The Ionian Mode accounts for a large proportion of traditional songs of which "Three Jolly Rogues of Lynn," "Barbara Allen" and "The Greenland Whale Fishery" are random examples.

The *Dorian Mode* begins on the same tonic note (C in our case) but its sequence is C,D,E ,F, G,A,B♭ ,C. It was considered to be the "Bestower of Wisdom and Chastity" and governed by the planet Saturn, which is echoed by its Arabic counterpart of *Maquâm Hijâx Kâr Kurd.* This mode is widespread in English folk songs such as "Souling Wassail," "Newlyn Town," "John Barleycorn" and even "What Shall We Do with the Drunken Sailor?," and its particular qualities are frequently mentioned in literature of the past, including John Milton's "Paradise Lost" which relates, " . . . Anon they move/In perfect phalanx to the Dorian mood of flutes and soft recorders."

The *Phrygian Mode* is C,D♭ ,E♭ ,F,G,A♭ ,B♭ ,C and was identified with Mars, as it "Causeth wars and enflameth fury." As such, music in this mode was played during the training of Spartan soldiers and on their way to battle. Its use in folksong is very rare; out of over 3,500 songs collected by Cecil Sharp in the British Isles and Appalachian Mountains he only discovered four, including the children's rhyme "Matthew, Mark, Luke and John, Bless the bed that I lie on," also known as "The White Paternoster." The Phrygian mode is, however, very characteristic of Spanish flamenco music with its Moorish origin.

The *Lydian Mode* of C,D,E,F♯ ,G,A,B,C was ruled by Jupiter and "Doth sharpen the wit of the dull and maketh them that are burdened with earthly cravings to desire heavenly things." For this reason, perhaps, it is widely used in plainchant, but out of the whole of traditional music is only known from one or two songs, including the ballad tune "The Woods So Wild" which dates back to the sixteenth century (when it was arranged for the virginals by William Byrd and the lute by Francis Cutting). John Milton refers to this mode in his poem "L'Allegro": "And ever against eating cares, lap me in soft Lydian airs."

The *Mixolydian Mode* was the ancient Major scale, only differing from the Ionian mode by its flatted seventh (C,D,E,F,G,A,B♭ ,C) and was associated with the sun. The unexpected flat note makes it very distinctive, particularly in songs such as "Blackwater Side" and the Scottish lament "Flowers of the Forest," where its appearance is delayed until near the end of each verse, the first of which occurs on the phrase "*Now* they are weeping, lamenting and sighing," creating a feeling of great poignancy. This mode is also the vehicle for many pipe and fiddle tunes, including "Bonaparte's Retreat," "The Little Beggarman" and "Old Joe Clark."

The *Aeolian Mode* is the normal minor scale of C,D,E♭ ,F,G,A♭ ,B♭ ,C. Its widespread use in many quiet and sad songs perhaps reflects its character of "Appeasing the tempests of the mind and lulling them asleep." Like the Dorian minor mode it occurs in many traditional songs such as "Searching for Lambs," "Scarborough Fair" or the beautiful "Bushes and Briars."

The *Locrian Mode* of C,D♭ ,E♭ ,F,G♭ ,A♭ ,B♭ ,C was known as a bastard scale due to the uneveness of its intervals and, being only of theorectical interest, was never used. There are no traditional songs within its compass, but two years ago a young folk musician called John Kirkpatrick made good use of its uneasy sound in his song "Ashes to Ashes," which tells the story of a grave-digger and has all the hallmarks of being absorbed into the traditional repertoire in the future.

Some songs and tunes are pentatonic (five note) or hexatonic (six note) so fall within the scope of two modes. The pentatonic scale is most often found in Celtic traditional music, as in the familar "Auld Lang Syne" or "Ye Banks and Braes" and in "The Seeds of Love," the first song collected by Cecil Sharp (who heard it sung in 1903 by a gardener aptly named John England).

These modes were a source of great surprise to the early folk song collectors, some of whom thought the tunes were incorrect, so notated them to conform to the standard major or minor scales and added quite unsuitable harmonies for accompaniment on the piano (which is never used in traditional music) to facilitate their performance in recitals, as a result totally destroying their unique character. Fortunately, however, later collectors such as The Reverend Baring Gould, Cecil Sharp, Percy Grainger, Ralph Vaughan Williams, and others realized the special qualities of these songs, which had existed almost unknown for generations, and took great pains to ensure that their modality was preserved in transcription.

As with other forms of modal music, folk song is entirely melodic and was normally performed unaccompanied. If an instrument were used it was normally restricted to doubling the melody and providing a drone; the drone being the tonic note of the mode and serving to emphasize its intervals as well as establishing the key note for the performer and listener. This is especially evident in Eastern music where its continuous sound is related to the basic pulse of life itself–the heartbeat. The popular use of the guitar in recent years to accompany folk songs is really quite inappropriate, as its chordal and chromatic basis is out of keeping with modal principles.

Because of the drone element direct comparisons can be made between the many forms of bagpipes, the dulcimer and its related instruments, the jaws harp, sitar, hurdy-gurdy, etc., all of which have origins in antiquity and are still used throughout the world to play modal music.

# Appendix B: Discography

**Albums Containing Tunes from This Book**

Most of the recordings are very close to the tunes which appear in the book.

Spence, Bill. *The Hammered Dulcimer.* Featuring Fennig's All-Star String Band. **Front Hall Records FHR-01.** Front Hall Records, R.D. 1, Wormer Rd., Voorheesville, N.Y. 12186.
*Contains:* "The Black Nag," "Childgrove," "Over The Waterfall" and "Rights of Man."

Russell, Bonnie. *The Russell Family.* Old-time instruments featuring Mountain Dulcimer playing. **County Records no. 734.** County Records, 307 E. 37th St., New York, N.Y. 10016.
*Contains:* "Fisher's Hornpipe," "Ebenezer," and "Silly Bill."

Roth, Kevin. *Kevin Roth Sings and Plays Dulcimer.* **Folkways FA 2367.** Folkways Records, 17 W. 60th St., New York, N.Y. 10023.
*Contains:* "Soldier's Joy," "Black Jack Davy" and "June Apple."

MacArthur, Margaret. *On the Mountains High.* **Living Folk Records F-LFR-100.** Living Folk Records, 65 Mt. Aubern St., Cambridge Mass. 02138.
*Contains:* "The Swallowtail Jig."

———. *The Old Songs.* **Philo Records-1001.**
*Contains:* "Jenny Lind Polka."

Pentangle, The. *Cruel Sister.* **Reprise-S6430.** Also *Solomon's Seal,* **Reprise S2100.**
*Contains:* "A Maid That's Deep in Love."

———. *Reflection.* **Reprise 6463.**
*Contains:* "Rain and Snow" and "The Wedding Dress Song."

Collins, Kathleen. *Kathleen Collins.* **Shanachie Records,** 1375 Crosby Ave., Bronx, N.Y. 10461.
*Contains:* "Band of Ireland" and "Tarbolton Lodge."

Prior, Maddy and Heart, Timmy. *Summer Solstice.* English Import. Can be found in a good folk record store, or: Thomas Stern, Box 1228, White Plains, N.Y. 10602.
*Contains:* "Bring Us In Good Ale" and "Serving Girl's Holiday."

Planxty. *Planxty* (1st Album). English Import. **Polydor Records.**
*Contains:* "Planxty Irwin."

———. *The Well Below the Valley.* **Polydor Records.**
*Contains:* "The Well Below The Valley."

Incredible String Band. *Liquid Acrobat as Regards the Air.* **Island Records 85749L.**
*Contains:* "Drops of Whiskey."

———. *The Hangmans Beautiful Daughter.* **Electra Records.**
*Contains:* "Everything's Fine Right Now."

Fairport Convention. *Full House.* **A & M S4265.**
*Contains:* "Flowers of the Forest" (a rather different version).

Fuzzy Mt. String Band. *Summer Oaks and Back Porches.*
*Contains:* "Lock Lavan Castle."

Watson, Doc. *The Doc. Watson Family.* **Vanguard Records.**
*Contains:* "Bonaparte's Retreat."

Bream, Julian. *The Woods So Wild.*
*Contains:* "The Woods So Wild."

Blake, Norman. *Whiskey Before Breakfast.*
*Contains:* "The Minstrel Boy to War Has Gone."

Pumpkin, Pied. *Pied Pumpkin Allah Mode.* 2104 Alberta Street, Vancouver, British Columbia, Canada.
*Contains:* "Tree."

Rubin, Dan. *Dan Rubin.* Write c/o: The Dill Pickle Rag, Box 66047, Station F, Vancouver, B.C., Canada V5N 5L4.
*Contains:* "Sea Wind."

Monroe, Bill. *Bluegrass Instrumentals.*
*Contains:* "Scotland."

Hollow Rock String Band. *Hollow Rock String Band.*
*Contains:* "Boatin' Up Sandy."

Smith, Ralph Lee. *Dulcimer Old Time and Traditional Music.* **Skyline Records**, Stephens City, Va. 22653.
*Contains:* "Cluck Old Hen."

Hellman, Neal; Carroll, Bonnie; Force, Robert; d'Ossché, Albert; and Rugg, Mike. Doing a joint dulcimer album to be released in the fall of 1977. **Biscuit City Records**, 1106 E. 17th Ave., Denver, Colo. 80218
*Contains:* "Marjorie," and might also contain: "Cornwall," "Poker Face Smile," "Farewell to Galapagos" and "Maggie in the Wood."

## Additional Discography

Anderson, Ila. *Ila Anderson.* **Audicom Records.** Available at J & F Records, listed below.

Armstrong, George and Gerry. *Simple Gifts.* **Folkways FLW 2335.**

Buckly, Bruce. *Ohio Valley Ballads.* **Folkways FLW 2025.**

Clayton, Paul. *Dulcimer Songs and Solos.* **Folkways FLW 3571.**

———. *Cumberland Mountain Folksongs.* **Folkways FLW 2007.**

Fairport Convention. *Angel Delight.* **A & M S4319.** *Full House.* **A & M S4265.** *Babbacombe Lee.* **A & M** All their others have some dulcimer; many of their tunes are suitable for the dulcimer.

Fariña, Richard and Mimi. *The Best of Mimi and Richard Fariña.* **Vanguard VSD-21/22.** Contains both their previous albums.

———. *Richard Fariña & Eric VanSchmidt* with "Blind Boy Grunt" (Dylan). **Vanguard Records.**

———. *Memories.* **Vanguard 79263.**

Hall, Kenny. *Kenny Hall.* **Philo Records.** Features Holly Tannen on dulcimer, from whom I hope a solo album will soon appear.

Mayan, Judy. *Folk Songs of Old Erie.* Order from Dulcimer Player News, P.O. Box 157, Front Royal, Va. 22630.

Mitchell, Howard and friends. *The Golden Ring.* **Folk-Legacy Records**, c/o Patton, Sharon, Conn. 06069

Mitchell, Joni. *Blue.* **Reprise S2038.** Also *Miles of Aisles.* (Reprise). Many of Joni's tunes are good for dulcimer because she plays the guitar in open tunings.

Proffitt, Frank. *Frank Proffitt.* **Folkways FLW 2360.**

Ritchie, Jean. *The Ritchie Family of Kentucky.* **Folkways FA 2316**

———. *British Traditional Ballads in the Southern Mountains.*(Vols. 1&2). **Folkways FA 2301 & 2302.**

Rolling Stones. *Aftermath.* **London PS-476.**

Simmons Family. *Wandering Through the Racksack.* Order from The Dulcimer Shoppe, Mountain View, Arkansas, 72560.

Schilling, Jean and Lee. *Old Traditions* and *Porches of the Poor.* Traditional records. Jean and Lee have many books, albums and other items as well. They also are the founders of The Folk Life Center Of The Smokies. Information on all the above can be obtained through: Jean and Lee Schilling, P.O. Box 8, Cosby, Tenn. 37722.

Steel-Eye-Span. Many albums on which the dulcimer is featured: *10-Man Mop, Pleased to See the King, Now We Are 6, Below the Salt* and *Parcel of Roques.* All can be found at decent record stores except *10-Man Mop;* try Cecil Sharp House, listed below.

Thompson, Richard and Linda. *I Wanna See the Bright Lights Tonight.* English import. Great Album. Try Cecil Sharp House.

Smith, Ralph Lee and Allen Block. *Ralph Lee Smith and Allen Block.* **Meadowlands Records**, 2301 Loring Place, Bronx, N.Y. 10468 ($3.75).

Rhodes, Mary. *The Dulcimer of Mary Rhodes.* French "Chant du Monde" series, **LDX 74485.**

# Appendix C: Bibliography

The following bibliography was compiled mainly from two sources: "A Bibliography of Hammered and Plucked (Appalachian or Mountain) Dulcimers and Related Instruments" by Joe Hickerson (c/o The Library of Congress Music Division, Archive of Folk Song, Washington D.C. 20540). Updated lists are *free* so just write for that and other related folk genres. I also used "The Complete Plucked Dulcimer Bibliography" compiled by Phillip Mason, The Dulcimer Player News, P.O. Box 157, Front Royal, Virginia 22630.

## Dulcimer Instruction Books


Hellman, Neal & Sally. *Life Is Like A Mountain Dulcimer.* New York: The Richmond Organization (10 Columbus Circle, N.Y. 10023) *Order from:* Songways Service, 17 W. 60th St., New York, NY 10023.

———. *The Richard Fariña Dulcimer Book.* New York: Gourd Music, 1977. *Order from:* Gourd Music, 8th floor, 17 W. 60th St., New York, NY 10023.

Force, Robert & d'Ossché, Albert. *In Search of the Wild Dulcimer.* New York: Random House, 1974. (Sold to Oak Publications, New York, NY 1975.)

Jeffreys, A.W. *Tuning and Playing the Appalachian Dulcimer.* Staunton, Va: Appalachian Dulcimer Co., 1964.

MacEachron, Len and Sue. *Playing the Dulcimer by Ear and Other Easy Ways.* Minneapolis: Here, Inc., 1970.

McSpadden, Lynn. *Four and Twenty Songs for the Mountain Dulcimer.* Mountain View, Ark.: Dulcimer Shoppe, 1970.

———. *Brethren We Have Met.* Same as above.

Mason, Phillip. *The Dulcimer Player's Bible.* Front Royal, Va: Dulcimer Player News, 1975.

———. *The Dulcimer Player News.* ($4.00 a year.) Phillip Mason, P.O. Box 157, Front Royal, Va., 22630.

Mitchell, Howard W. *The Mountain Dulcimer–How to Make It and Play It (After a Fashion).* Sharon, Conn. 06069: Folk-Legacy Records (FS129), 1966. Record and book.

Murphy, Michael. *The Appalachian Dulcimer Book.* Ohio: Folksay Press, 1976.

Nicholson, Roger (Edited and transcribed by John Pearse) *Nonesuch for Dulcimer.* London: Scratchwood Music, 1972. A book of tablature to accompany a record of the same name. Order from: Leader Sound Ltd., 5 North Villas, London, N.W. England. Record no.: **Trailer 3034**.

———. A second album and book: *Musick's Delight on the Dulcimer* or *The New Elizabethan* (book), and the record: *The Gentle Sound of the Dulcimer.* London: Argo Record Co., **Argo ZDA 204**. Scratchwood Music is distributed by EMI Music Publishing Ltd., 138/140 Charing Cross Road, London WC2H OLD. Mr. Nicholson will have a 3rd album and book out soon. *Times and Traditions for Dulcimer* (**Trailer 2094**). They are all excellent; a must for fingerpickers and lovers of Celtic music.

Pearse, John. *The Dulcimer Book.* London: A.T.V. Kirshner Music, Welback Music, Ltd. (Centuary 21 House, May's Court, St. Martin's Lane, London W.C.2, England), 1970.

———. *Teach Yourself the Appalachian Dulcimer.* London: English Folk Dance and Song Society, 1966.

Putnam, John F. *The Plucked Dulcimer of the Southern Mountains.* Berea, Kentucky: Council of the Southern Mountains, 1961.

Ritchie, Jean. *The Dulcimer Book.* New York: Oak Publications, 1963.

———. *Jean Ritchie's Dulcimer People.* New York: Oak Publications, 1975.

Schecter, Martha. *Dulcimer Tuning.* Cambridge, Mass: M. Schecter (Rm. 14 N-211, M.I.T.), 1970.

Smith, Ralph Lee. *Some Pointers for Beginning Dulcimer Players.* "Sing Out!" Vol. 20, No. 2, Nov.-Dec. 1970, pp. 6-9.

Winters, Margaret. *How to Play the Dulcimer.* Boston: Boston Music Co., 1963.

# Appendix D: Sources for Books and Records

Many have already been given with the above list. Here are some more:

*Folkways Records,* 701 7th Ave., New York, N.Y. 10036.

*Capritaurus Dulcimers,* P.O. Box 153, Felton, California 95018. Books and records.

*Folk-Legacy Records.* c/o Patton, Sharon, Conn. 06069.

*The Folk Shop.* Cecil Sharp House, 2 Regents Park Rd., NW1 7Ay-England. They have a lot of your hard-to-get English albums.

*J & F Record Sales,* 4501 Risinghill Road, Altadena Calif. 91001. They carry a lot of imports.

*Andys Front Hall,* RD1 Wormer Rd. Voorheesville, N.Y. 12186.

And of course, you can always try your local library.

### Books that contain tunes suitable for Dulcimer arrangement.

Most of the tunes in this book, plus others of the same genre, can be found in:

*The Kerr's Collection of Merry Melodies* (Vols. 1,2,3 and 4) Scottish and Irish Reels and Jigs, Highland Schottisches, Country Dances, Hornpipes, Waltzes, Polkas, Clog Dances, etc. They are $1.50 each, or $6.00 for the set; 450 tunes to a book. Order from: *The Fiddle Shop,* 304 Lakeside Avenue South, Seattle, Washington, WA 98144 (they also have a great collection of books and albums, including all the *Chieftan* albums).

Bruce, Collingwood J. and Stoke, John, (eds.) *Northumbrian Minstrelsy.* Detroit: Gale Research Co., 1882.

Chappell, William. *Old English Popular Music* (2 vols.). London: Chappell, 1893.

Child, Francis J. (ed.). *The English and Scottish Popular Ballads.* (5 vols.). New York: Dover Publ., 1882-1898. Reprint.

Lomax, John and Alan. *American Ballads and Folk Songs.* New York: The Macmillan Co., 1934.
———.*Folk Song U.S.A.* New York: Duell, Sloan and Pearce, 1947.

*O'Neill's Music of Ireland.* Revised by Miles Krassen. New York: Oak Publications, 1976.

Sharp Cecil. *English Folk Songs from the Southern Appalachians* (2 vols.). London: Oxford, 1932, 1952.

Stapleton, Olaf. *Last and First Men/Star Maker.* New York: Dover (reprint). Two of the greatest science fiction novels of all time. (Only $2.50.) A must for the dulcimer player who has everything.

Whall, W.D. *Ships, Seas, Songs and Shanties.* Glasgow: James Brown, 1912.

# Other great dulcimer books you'll want to try

**The Dulcimer Book**
**by Jean Ritchie**
Words and music for 16 songs from the Ritchie Family of Kentucky. Plus: how to tune and play; recollections on the dulcimer's local history; observations on its origins; and plenty of illustrations and drawings.
$2.95

**The Appalachian Dulcimer Book**
**by Michael Murphy**
Everything needed for playing and appreciation of the Appalachian dulcimer: history and folklore; instructions for playing, including discussion of modal music; how to read music; picks and noters; strumming; chord charts; classic tunes with lyrics; buying and repairing a dulcimer; discography and many rare photos.
$4.95

**In Search of the Wild Dulcimer**
**by Robert Force and Albert d'Ossché**
This one-of-a-kind guide explains everything about getting a good dulcimer, learning to play it, adapting its simple sounds to more complex, contemporary styles and playing the dulcimer with guitar. It starts by introducing elementary terms, rhythm, and musical modal systems; moves on to picking, chording, and melodic structure; and ends with a section of further source material and quick reference charts. Beautifully illustrated. "In its thoroughness, detail and respect for the history and tradition of the instrument, the book should well serve anyone who wants to learn to play. ... It's the next best thing to getting it first hand." *New Age Journal.*
$3.95

**Merrily Strum: Mountain Dulcimer for Children**
**by Mary Catherine McSpadden**
Twenty-three favorite children's songs with simple instructions for playing on the mountain dulcimer. A perfect beginner's guide which will make playing easy. Photos show how a child learns to play. Favorites (with words) include "Farmer in the Dell," "Bill Grogan's Goat" and "Hush Little Baby."
$2.50

**Jean Ritchie's Dulcimer People**
Friends here contribute their dulcimer experiences, news, memories, snapshots, playing styles, tuning and tablature methods, favorite songs, opinions, advice and information on where-to-buy, how-to-build, and where-to-listen-to the Appalachian dulcimer.
$4.95

Available at your local music store or directly from: Amsco Music Publishing Co. Dept. BA, 33 West 60th Street, New York 10023. Please add 50¢ per order for postage and handling. Send for our handsome, illustrated catalog FREE.